"AI didn't give me more time—it helped me turn intuition into better decisions. In *Artificial Organizations*, Barry O'Reilly guides leaders on how to achieve that in a way that's both practical and deeply human."

> **—Misty Shafer Sterne,** VP of Commercial Technology at American Airlines

"*Artificial Organizations* cuts through the AI noise, providing leaders with a clear, practical path from curiosity to confident action. It's already transforming how I approach my board cycle."

> **—David Gledhill,** Non-Executive Director of Singapore Airlines and Santander UK

"AI doesn't replace executive judgment—it raises the standard for it. *Artificial Organizations* shows leaders how to meet that standard."

> **—Joe Noreña,** former COO of Global Markets Americas at HSBC

"AI is only as powerful as the operating model around it. *Artificial Organizations* shows leaders how to embed AI into the rhythm of decision-making—so speed increases without sacrificing judgment."

> **—Steve Elliot,** CEO and Founder of Dotwork

"Barry O'Reilly cuts through the AI hype and demonstrates how leaders can use AI as a true thinking partner—sharpening judgment, clarifying strategy, and scaling impact with confidence."

> **—Steven Leist,** CTO of Progyny

"AI doesn't replace leaders, it reveals the quality of their thinking. In *Artificial Organizations*, Barry O'Reilly delivers a practical blueprint for sharper judgment, faster decisions, and stronger results in an AI-enabled world."

> **—Dr. Edward J. Hoffman,** former Chief Knowledge Officer and Director of NASA Academy

"Finally, a book about AI that's actually about leadership."

> **—Eric Ries,** author of *The Lean Startup* and *Incorruptible*

ARTIFICIAL ORGANIZATIONS

Build Better Judgment, Speed, and Results with Human and Machine Intelligence

Barry O'Reilly

For information about bulk purchases, corporate sales, or special editions, please contact: www.artificialorganizations.com

Published in the United States by Barry O'Reilly, www.barryoreilly.com

ISBN: 978-1-0676263-2-7
Library of Congress Control Number: 1-15112780071

First Edition

Printed in the United States of America

10 9 8 7 6 5 4 3 2 1

Disclaimer
The information contained in this book is for educational and informational purposes only. While every effort has been made to ensure accuracy, the author and publisher make no representations or warranties regarding the completeness or suitability of the information provided. The strategies and examples discussed may not be appropriate for every individual or organization. Readers are responsible for their own decisions and actions.

References to specific companies, tools, products, or services do not constitute endorsement unless explicitly stated.

To Oscar and Liam

*May the future inspire you,
as you have inspired me.*

CONTENTS

ACKNOWLEDGMENTS

This book was not written in isolation. It was shaped in conversations, in workshops, in boardrooms, in moments of pressure, and in the quiet reflections that followed.

First, to the leaders I've had the privilege of working alongside over the past few years. Many of you are navigating extraordinary complexity within companies such as American Airlines, Atlassian, AWS, Capital One, Dotwork, HSBC, Progyny, Skyscanner, Spotify, Slack, Wells Fargo, and many others. You're making consequential decisions with incomplete information, compressed timelines, and constant visibility.

Artificial Organizations exists because of the questions you were brave enough to ask out loud:

- How do I think clearly again?
- How do we move faster without breaking trust?
- What should remain human?
- Where should we let the machine lead?

You allowed me into your work arenas—not the polished facades, but the actual places where difficult decisions are made. The stories, systems, and case studies in this book are grounded in your real challenges under pressure. Thank you for trusting me to be there with you.

To my team, Sham Colegado and Trisha Famor, thank you for your tireless work, positive energy, and pursuit of excellence in all that you do. People still do not believe how such a small team can make such an outsized impact.

To the crew at Nobody Studios, thank you for living this work, trying to figure out how to build 100 AI companies together, and persisting in the face of the odds.

To my reviewers: Andrew Phillips, Cassandra Pratt, Chris Ng, Christian Blunden, Diana Kander, Eric Ries, Jeff Gothelf, Joe Noreña,

John Marcante, John Snel, Jonny Schneider, Kyle Byrd, Martin Eriksson, Maryam Aidini, Misty Shafer Sterne, Niall O'Reilly, Pete Anevski, Peter Faulhaber, Richard Lennox, Rohit Jain, Sabrina Braham, Secil Tabli Watson, Stephen Franchetti, Stephen O'Reilly, Steve Elliot, Steven Leist, Tanya Cordrey, Teresa Torres, and Tristan Fagan. You've pushed my thinking, challenged my assumptions, and refused easy answers. This book is better because of you.

To my editor Casey Ebro, my collaborator Peter Economy, my production manager Steve Straus, and all the challengers of these ideas. You demanded evidence, examples, and a practical path for others to apply AI. That insistence made this work sharper and more useful.

To my family, especially Qiu Yi. Writing a book is invisible work over a long time. It's early mornings, late nights, and half-finished chats because a thought had to be captured. Thank you for your patience, your encouragement, and the grounding perspective I needed.

Finally, to the leaders standing at a threshold right now. You can feel it. The systems that brought you here will not carry you forward. The volume of information will not slow down. The pressure will not disappear. The tools will only grow more powerful.

Artificial Organizations is the product of hundreds of hours spent in that tension between human and machine, between promise and concern. Such productive dissent and dialogue shaped the central idea of this book: that the future does not belong to humans alone or machines alone but to those who learn to leverage both.

Here's the opportunity: You get to design what comes next. You get to decide how human and machine intelligence work together for you, and within your organization. You get to shape judgment infrastructure, feedback loops, and operating rhythms that elevate human judgment rather than overwhelm it. You get to build cultures that are both deeply human and technologically forward.

That work is not theoretical. It's happening already, and it requires leaders who are willing to question old assumptions, experiment responsibly, and stay steady in the face of change.

It is my hope that this book helps you build an organization that thinks more clearly, adapts more fluidly, and performs more responsibly. Thank you for being part of that journey.

t was just after midnight when I realized something was broken. Not the work. Not my ambition. Not my capability. It was the way I was working.

The house was quiet. My family asleep. Dinner untouched. I was alone at my desk—again—rewriting a business case that should have been finished days earlier.

On the surface, everything looked like success: advising CEOs and leadership teams, building companies, speaking on innovation, juggling more opportunities than I could reasonably say yes to. Yet inside, it felt different. It felt frustrating.

I wasn't physically tired. I was mentally overloaded. Reactive. Carrying too many decisions in my head, with no space to think them through properly.

What unsettled me most wasn't the workload itself. It was the growing sense that **despite more tools, more data, and more intelligence than ever before, my decisions weren't getting easier.** They were getting harder—and heavier.

Judgment Under Pressure

Every executive I work with describes the same experience, even if they use different words:

"I don't have time to think anymore."

They're smart, experienced, and capable. Yet they're constantly interrupted—pulled from meeting to meeting, drowning in dashboards, instant messages, and updates—while the decisions they're responsible for only get bigger, harder, and more consequential.

For years, leaders were told that more information, better tools, and greater efficiency would create leverage. Instead, many found themselves buried under complexity. Decision cycles slowed. Context fragmented. Presence eroded.

We now live in a strange paradox:

* more data than ever

* more compute power than ever

* more intelligence everywhere

But the result isn't clarity. It's noise. **Judgment is overburdened.**

Leaders can't discern if their organizations are losing because of bad strategy, poor choices, or faulty information. The truth is, they lose because decisions move too slowly through the system.

Compounding this, executives' feeds are now full of promises: *This tool will fix your meetings. This bot will automate your workflow. This platform will keep you competitive.* It's Fear of Missing Out (FOMO) messaging that warns if you don't move fast enough, you're falling behind.

As the world grows ever more complex and uncertain, human leadership is being called upon more than ever. Yes, machines are extraordinary. They can process, store, and compute at a scale no human ever could—instantly, cheaply, relentlessly. What they cannot do is be you—with your imagination, your unique instincts, skills, and experiences to make creative human decisions.

Machines are excellent at processing information, but they are terrible at deciding what matters. That responsibility still lies with you.

The constraint in AI-augmented leadership is no longer information. It is judgment under pressure.

The Night I Stopped Trying to Work Faster

That night at my desk, I didn't decide to become more productive. I decided to stop working the way I always had.

Instead of asking, How do I do more?, I asked:

* How do I make my best decisions?

* Which aspects of my work confuse my thinking rather than sharpen it?

* What activities genuinely require my involvement as a leader?

I wrote everything down—patterns, energy spikes, friction points, blind spots—and quickly realized:

My highest-value leadership moments weren't about execution. They were about judgment.

Those moments took place during high-stakes conversations, decision forums, and meetings where clarity and presence mattered far more than speed. Yet those moments were often diluted by low-leverage tasks—preparation, capture, and synthesis—that pulled my attention away from the work only I could do.

I ran a small experiment that involved *one behavior change*. I introduced a machine as an assistant, starting with meetings. It could listen without bias, capture without distraction, and synthesize without fatigue. That way, I could do what was most important as a leader: **be fully present.**

What Changed Wasn't Efficiency. It Was Authority.

As the machine captured more information, my output accelerated. Preparation took minutes instead of hours. Follow-ups became clearer. Context stopped leaking. But the real shift wasn't productivity. It was how I showed up.

I walked into conversations calmer. My decisions felt grounded instead of rushed. I stopped carrying everything in my head.

People noticed. Colleagues commented on the clarity of outcomes, and wanted to work together. Executives remarked on how discussions were more efficient, more insightful, and, most importantly, more decisive. Teams moved faster—not because I pushed harder, but because ambiguity disappeared.

The machine didn't replace me. It supported me. It gave me space to think, empowered my decisions, and enabled me to be fully present when it mattered most. I felt I was doing the best work of my life, and I was having fun doing it.

That's when it became clear: AI isn't primarily a productivity tool. It enables a **judgment system**. Used well, it makes leaders better. Authority increases.

This is not automation. It is judgment infrastructure.

Most organizations add AI at the edges. Artificial Organizations redesign the core.

What This Book Is Really About . . .

This is not a book about tools, technology, or how you're going to be replaced.

It's about **how leaders think, decide, and lead when you combine human *and* machine intelligence.**

You'll learn how to design a personal AI operating system that will help you:

* improve decision quality under pressure
* increase decision velocity without sacrificing judgment
* create space for strategic thinking

AI becomes a trusted thinking partner that will:

* clarify half-formed ideas
* pressure test strategies
* explore scenarios
* prepare you for critical conversations

This book presents practical systems grounded in real leadership work, tested with executives who shoulder real responsibility and real consequences, all informed by case studies from Amazon, American Airlines, Dotwork, HSBC, Progyny, Skyscanner, Slack, and the global Top 10 AI venture studio[1] I co-founded, Nobody Studios.

. . . And What It's Designed to Do

This book moves in three deliberate steps.

First, we focus on you. How leaders reduce cognitive load, build a personal Judgment System, and use AI to think more clearly under pressure.

---

1. Startup Savant, 12 Top Venture Studios for Startups in 2026 https://startupsavant .com/best-venture-studios.

Then we scale outward. How you, and in turn your teams, build Judgment Infrastructure—capturing work as data, synthesizing signal from noise, and accelerating alignment without adding bureaucracy.

Finally, we look at advantage. How faster, clearer decisions compound into execution momentum, strategic resilience, and long-term competitive edge.

This is not a book about tools. It's about redesigning how judgment works—so speed increases without sacrificing clarity, and performance compounds instead of stalls.

AI transformation follows a predictable progression:

**Personal Productivity → Executive Workflows →
Departmental Pilots → Organizational Scale**

This book focuses on the first two stages—Personal Productivity and Executive Workflows—because departmental and organizational transformation **don't work if you skip the personal transformation.**

If you haven't redesigned how *you* think, decide, and lead with AI, any attempt to scale it across teams, departments, and the organization will fail. According to a major study from the Massachusetts Institute of Technology (MIT) Networked Agents and Decentralized AI (NANDA) initiative[2], when enterprise leaders roll out GenAI pilots without redesigning how work flows and how judgment is incorporated, **approximately 95% of those efforts produce no measurable business value or sustained P&L impact**, with **only about 5% of projects scaling into production** and delivering meaningful results.

The leaders who succeed don't start with mandates. They begin by changing how they work, and role model AI adoption themselves.

I wrote this book to help you create **personal leadership systems—** for thinking, preparation, and decision-making—that will take you **from Productivity to Performance and then Presence.**

---

2. Massachusetts Institute of Technology. The GenAI Divide: State of AI in Business 2025. NANDA Initiative report, July 2025.

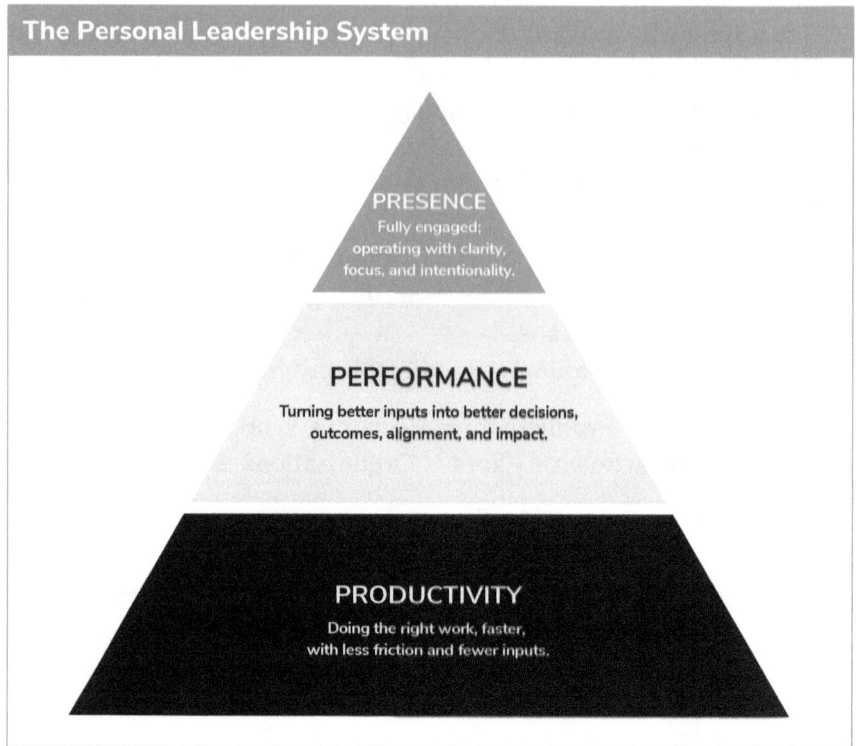

The goal isn't to become an AI expert. It's to become a **more effective leader**, who exhibits clarity of thought, makes better decisions, and navigates uncertain environments with greater confidence.

This work changed how I lead, how I decide, and how I show up—at work and at home. My hope is that it does the same for you.

As you begin this leadership journey, you may recognize habits that once served you well—and now hold you back. That discomfort isn't failure. It's the signal that you must unlearn past success to achieve extraordinary results. I challenge you to think big and start small. Then stack skills and scale over time.

Leaders in your industry are already shortening their decision cycles and compounding advantage.

Will you be among them?

PART I

THE JUDGMENT CONSTRAINT

**"If AI doesn't change behavior,
it's decoration."**

Organizations are investing heavily in intelligence, yet senior leaders are not experiencing greater clarity. Dashboards multiply. Output accelerates. Outcomes have not kept pace. Decision latency compounds. Context fractures across meetings and channels. Reversals consume time and credibility.

The constraint is not access to information. It is judgment capacity. In this part, you will examine decision velocity and decision advantage, and confront where speed is masking structural weaknesses. You will see how fragmented context increases cognitive drag and how unstructured decisions erode authority over time.

Before you install Judgment Infrastructure, you must understand what is slowing you down.

CHAPTER 1

YOUR LEGACY IS NOW YOUR LIABILITY

*What is most important isn't who knows
the answer, but who knows how to get
the answer, from where, fastest.*

For decades, leadership advantage came from experience. You rose because you could spot patterns faster than others, because you carried institutional memory, and because you made good judgment calls under pressure when information was incomplete. Those strengths built your career. Today, they no longer scale.

Experience used to compound automatically over time. In the age of AI, experience only compounds if it is augmented. Otherwise, it calcifies.

For the first time in history, leaders now operate alongside systems that can recall more context, synthesize more information, and test more scenarios than any individual human ever could. The shift isn't simply automation, it's better judgment.

Good leaders aren't outsourcing their decisions. They're **augmenting how they make decisions**.

This creates two forces:

- **decision velocity**—how quickly you move from *question →
insight → decision → action*

- **decision advantage**—how informed, accurate, and context-rich those decisions are

Speed without insight creates chaos, while insight without speed results in irrelevance. When decision velocity and decision advantage compound together, leadership itself changes shape.

Leaders who combine human instinct with machine-supported insight aren't just moving faster. They're making *better* decisions—consistently. This is where the gap between those who augment their judgment and compound advantage, and those who don't widens exponentially.

What 5,000 Leaders Revealed

In July 2025, I surveyed my mailing list of over **5,000 senior leaders**—CEOs, C-suite executives, VPs, and Directors—on how they were actually using AI.

The results were telling:

- **61%** described themselves as beginners
- only **4%** considered themselves experts (most people overestimate their skills in surveys)
- **over 52% of usage involved low-level tasks**: emails, document drafts, and light experimentation after hours

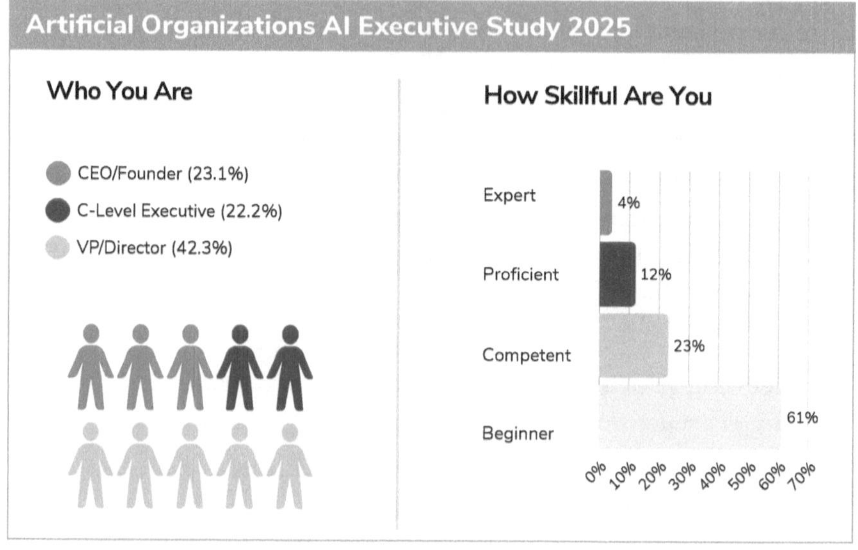

How senior leaders wanted to learn was also revealing:

- **35%** preferred 1:1 coaching
- **42%** favored small peer cohorts
- only **10%** were interested in workshop or on-demand courses

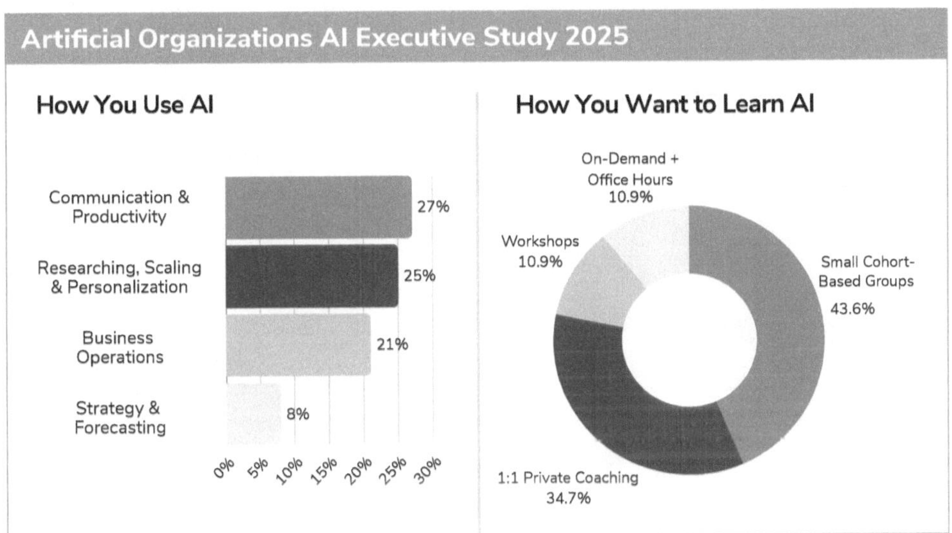

As I worked with senior leaders, it became clear why an overwhelming majority preferred smaller learning environments. They were all extremely competent, curious, and willing to learn, but they lacked the psychological safety to experiment publicly—especially with a technology they felt immense pressure to understand.

The signal was unmistakable: **Being a beginner at the top is uncomfortable. Feeling incompetent is even worse.**

When I compared the priorities of CEOs (financial incentive owners) versus VPs and Directors (delivery execution owners) the most important insights emerged. I asked what each party believed is the biggest ROI from AI.

- **45% of CEOs** said cost reduction and efficiency
- **37% of VPs and Directors** focused on time relief and burnout alleviation

- only **13%** across both groups prioritized the highest-leverage outcome of all: **better decisions, faster**

That's the blind spot. And it's where the advantage is already compounding for leaders combining human and machine intelligence for better judgment, speed, and results.

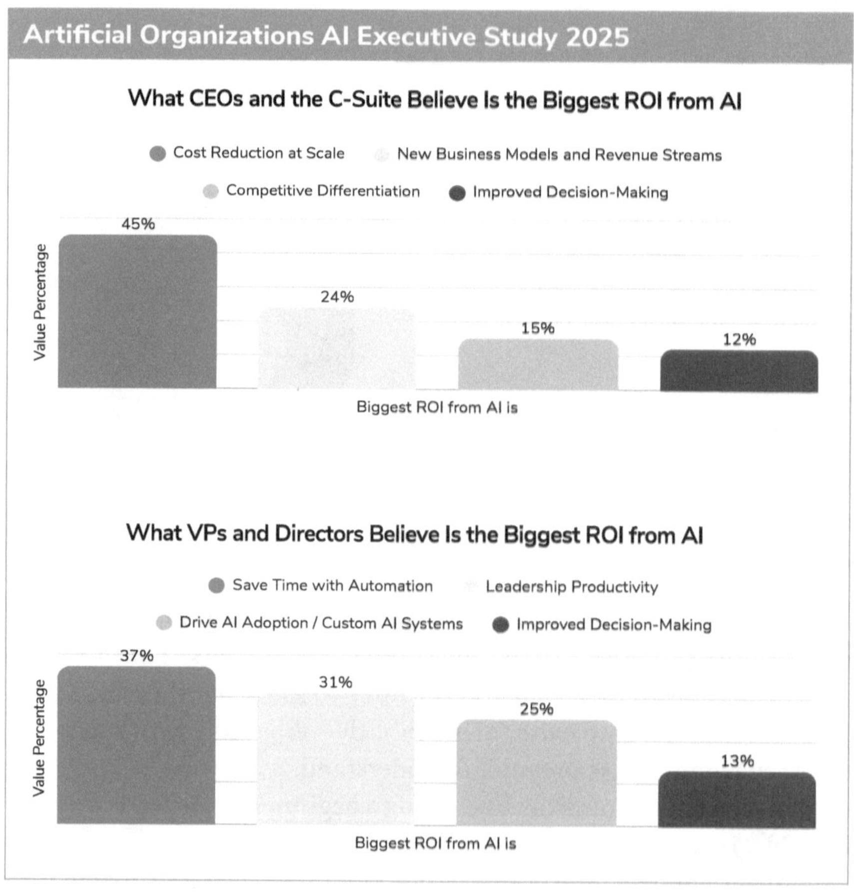

The 80/20 Mismatch Most Leaders Miss

I asked leaders to map their actual time, and discovered a striking pattern.

Roughly 80% of leadership time is consumed by:

* meetings
* updates
* coordination
* administration
* reconstructing context

Yet 80% of leadership value is created by:

* framing the right problems
* evaluating trade-offs
* being fully present in critical moments
* making high-quality decisions

This isn't a time management issue. It's a decision allocation problem, and until you redesign how judgment flows, no AI tool will save you.

I challenged leaders:

* What percentage of your time is spent solving hard problems, doing high-value work that only you can do?
* What percentage of your time is being eaten away by low-leverage, yet necessary time-sucking tasks?
* What would happen if you could shift those ratios by 5%, 10%, even 50% to have more time focused on creative problem-solving?

Do this thought experiment right now. Your answers may shock you.

Legacy leadership rewards responsiveness. Today, leadership demands judgment augmented by AI.

From Linear Leadership to Exponential Innovation

To understand how deep this leadership shift is, look at how value creation has changed.

The Most Valuable Companies at the Beginning of Each Decade		
2000	**2010**	**2020**
Microsoft	Exxon	Apple
General Electric	General Electric	Amazon
Exxon	Microsoft	Microsoft
Shell	AT&T	Alphabet
Merck	Procter and Gamble	Facebook

In 2000, the world's most valuable companies scaled through:

* people
* assets

- hierarchy
- geographic expansion
- being #1 in your market

By 2010, very little had changed. Leaders had a very linear view of the world, believing that what made them successful in the past would work in the future.

Then by 2020, that logic collapsed—and everything changed. Companies like Apple, Amazon, Alphabet, and Meta didn't scale by adding people. They scaled with technology.

They **built judgment infrastructure**—platforms that learned faster than competitors about how customers used their products and services, what features worked, and what features didn't—at massive volume, precision, and accuracy.

One question I often ask executives: How many people do you think run Apple Pay? Most guess thousands. The answer is closer to fifty—serving billions.

This didn't happen because those leaders worked harder. It happened because they redesigned how decisions were made.

I've recognized this pattern multiple times through the internet, mobile, and cloud computing eras.

In 2010, I remember encouraging financial institutions to adopt cloud computing. People told me they would never give up their servers. Too risky. Too much compliance. Too little control that they didn't want to hand over to another entity.

At the same time, one of my *Lean Enterprise*[1] co-authors Jez Humble was releasing *Continuous Delivery*,[2] his book with Dave Farley, which explained how companies could ship software thousands of times a day using automated tests, development pipelines, and cloud infrastructure.

We advised leaders to release software hundreds of times a day. They thought we were insane.

Why?

---

1. Jez Humble, Joanne Molesky, and Barry O'Reilly, *Lean Enterprise: How High Performance Organizations Innovate at Scale* (Sebastopol, CA: O'Reilly Media, 2014).
2. Jez Humble and David Farley, *Continuous Delivery: Reliable Software Releases through Build, Test, and Deployment Automation* (Boston: Addison-Wesley, 2010).

Because they had mapped everything they needed to do to release software—a series of steps that took weeks, months, even years in some cases—and wondered how they could do the same in minutes.

By 2013, *Amazon was deploying software every seven seconds*, while competitors shipped a few times a year[3].

It wasn't magic. It was a decision velocity and decision advantage engine in action.

Amazon was making better decisions than everyone else. It was learning faster, iterating more frequently, and adapting.

AI is the next exponential innovation curve. And we are only at the beginning.

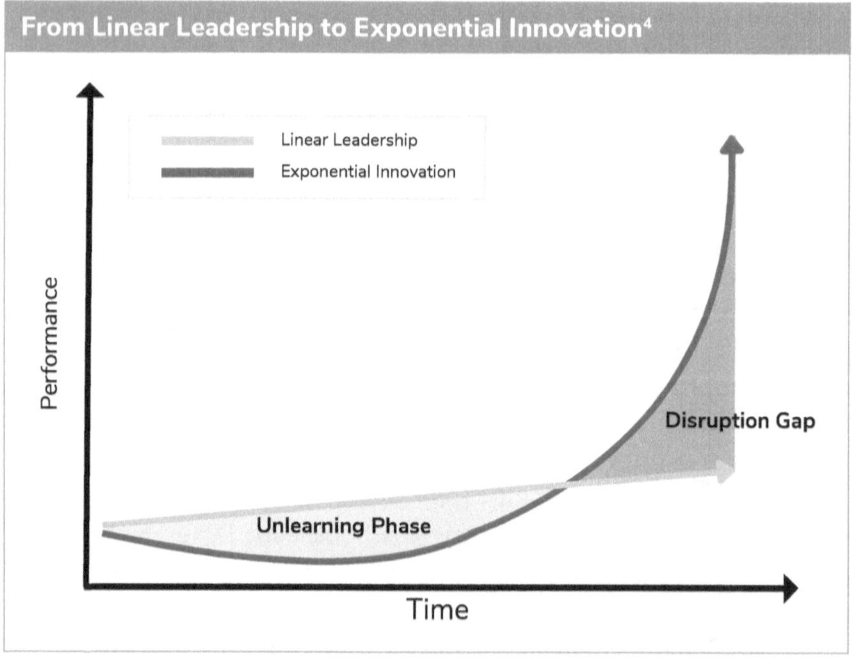

---

3. John Rossman, *The Amazon Way: 14 Leadership Principles Behind the World's Most Disruptive Company* (New York: McGraw-Hill Education, 2014).
4. Diagram inspired by Ray Kurzweil's Law of Accelerating Returns, the foundational theory behind his prediction of a Technological Singularity, a future point of rapid, uncontrollable technological growth—specifically artificial intelligence—that will fundamentally transform human civilization.

Most leaders stay on the linear leadership path—refining what already works, improving incrementally, and protecting the systems that made them successful. It feels safe and productive.

But innovation doesn't move linearly. It follows an exponential curve. Early on, progress looks slower and even deceptive. New behaviors feel awkward. Performance may dip. But once leaders unlearn, redesign how they work and integrate new capabilities, improvement compounds. The widening space between these two curves is the disruption gap.

Linear leadership optimizes yesterday. Exponential innovation redesigns tomorrow. One path improves the past. The other builds the future. The gap between them is where leaders are disrupted or pull ahead.

The Silent Killer: Decision Latency

According to McKinsey's 2025 *State of AI* report[5], **AI is now table stakes**:

- **90%** of organizations use AI

- **88%** say accelerating adoption is a priority

- **less than 40% see measurable Earnings Before Interest and Taxes (EBIT) gains**, and most report improvements under only **5%**

Adoption is everywhere, urgency is high, but material bottom-line returns remain modest. Access to AI is no longer the differentiator. **Leadership behavior is.**

Across organizations, I see the same three failure patterns appear again and again:

1. **Meeting-centric cultures**
   Context is rebuilt weekly. Decisions drift. Energy drains. AI collapses this by capturing context automatically, synthesizing insight instantly, and shortening meetings to decisions only.

---

5. McKinsey & Company, The State of AI in 2025: Agents, Innovation, and Transformation, McKinsey Global Survey on AI (November 2025).

2. **Overreliance on instinct**

   Experience still matters, but instinct alone loses to leaders with broader recall and deeper synthesis. In short, human instinct + machine insight = better outcomes.

3. **Hierarchy drag**

   Approvals, hand-offs, and delays persist in systems designed for a slower world. Leaders with judgment systems augmented with AI push decisions to the right level because information arrives ready— not weeks later. If you're leading the same way you did two years ago, you're already behind.

From Legacy Organizations to Artificial Organizations

When leaders deliberately combine human and machine intelligence to redesign how judgment flows through a company, the result is an **Artificial Organization**—one that moves faster, decides more clearly, and compounds advantage over time.

At the individual level, this begins with a **Judgment System**: a repeatable way a leader captures, synthesizes, decides, and acts using AI as a thinking partner.

At the organizational level, this scales into **Judgment Infrastructure**: the structural architecture that ensures decision quality improves as speed increases across teams.

Most companies bolt AI onto the edges of existing workflows. Artificial organizations redesign the core.

The shift is not about adding tools. It is about redesigning how context is captured, how signals are synthesized, and how decisions are executed.

The Architecture of an Artificial Organization diagram shows how intelligence compounds inside an organization—and how you can design that system deliberately.

The Architecture of an Artificial Organization

From Overload to Compounding Advantage

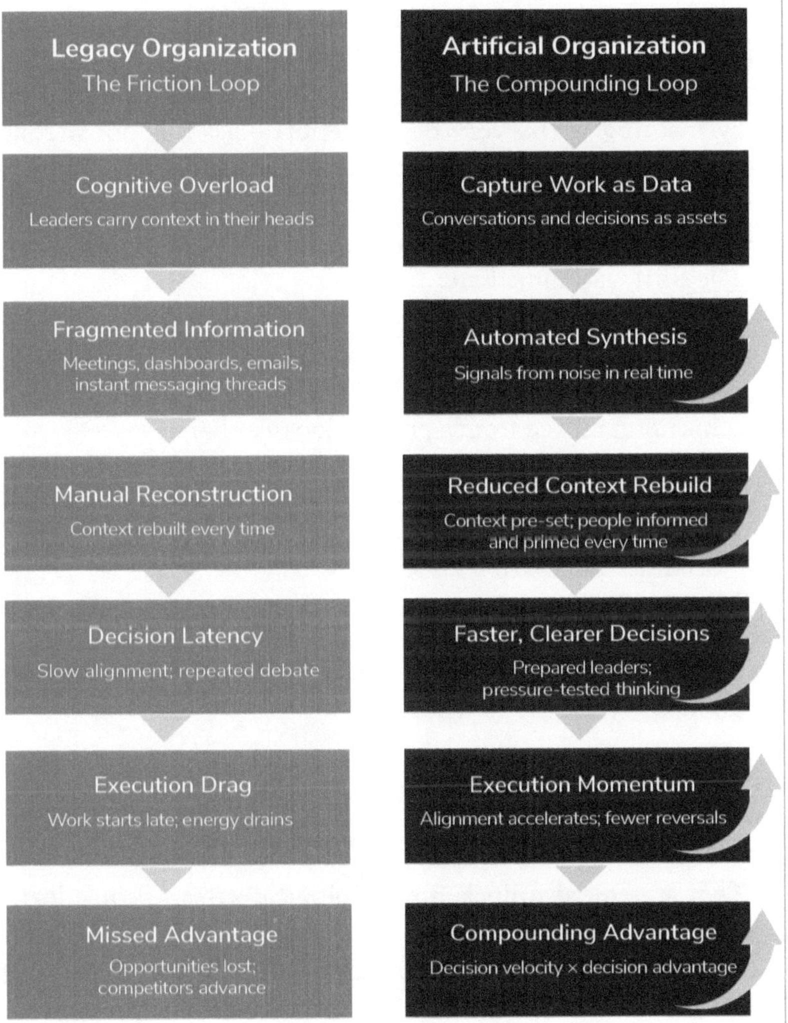 Legacy Organization	Artificial Organization
Legacy Organization The Friction Loop	**Artificial Organization** The Compounding Loop
Cognitive Overload Leaders carry context in their heads	**Capture Work as Data** Conversations and decisions as assets
Fragmented Information Meetings, dashboards, emails, instant messaging threads	**Automated Synthesis** Signals from noise in real time
Manual Reconstruction Context rebuilt every time	**Reduced Context Rebuild** Context pre-set; people informed and primed every time
Decision Latency Slow alignment; repeated debate	**Faster, Clearer Decisions** Prepared leaders; pressure-tested thinking
Execution Drag Work starts late; energy drains	**Execution Momentum** Alignment accelerates; fewer reversals
Missed Advantage Opportunities lost; competitors advance	**Compounding Advantage** Decision velocity × decision advantage

Underlying Leadership Model

- Memory-based leadership
- Meeting-heavy coordination
- Hierarchy bottlenecks
- Instinct under pressure

Underlying Leadership Model

- Judgment infrastructure
- Decision engines
- Learn and build in public
- Human and machine intelligence

Case Study: To Elevate, Not Eliminate
Pete Anevski, CEO of Progyny

Pete Anevski is the CEO of Progyny, a NASDAQ-listed leader in fertility and family building benefits and former CFO of WebMD. He's meticulous, detail-oriented, and deeply data-driven.

For years, he maintained a single Word document tracking every meeting with every direct report—risks, actions, concerns, commitments—updating it manually at the end of each day.

When we started working together, we began simply: **add an AI meeting assistant to each of his 1:1s.**

The shift was immediate:

- crisp synthesis of every conversation
- actions, owners, and due dates captured automatically
- his notes moved from a private doc to a shared space
- the team gained visibility
- decision cycles shortened
- accuracy improved
- headspace increased

But the defining leadership moment wasn't operational. It was when Pete announced to the company:

> **"We're not using AI to reduce headcount.**
> **We're using it to amplify your human skills.**
> **To elevate, not eliminate you and your work."**

That statement unlocked psychological safety. People leaned in. Experimentation exploded.

Then Pete asked the uncomfortable—but transformative—question: "What will you do with the capacity this creates?"

Most people assume capacity means "more work", "management will try to squeeze more out of us", or "give us greater workloads."

But the real opportunity isn't giving you more to do. It's giving you back more time to *think* creativity and strategically and to reflect in order to make better decisions with deeper insight.

You don't get better decisions by putting people under more pressure or on a faster hamster wheel. You get better decisions by giving people space to consider, process, and make tough choices with clarity, confidence, and conviction. Setting this expectation is the role of leadership, as modeled by Pete and Progyny.

Disruption Happens to People, Not Organizations

Organizations don't get disrupted. People do. Just as features must evolve for products to stay relevant in the market, leaders must evolve their behaviors. Relying on past systems, hoping you'll succeed in the future is not the right path. You must unlearn, to relearn and grow.

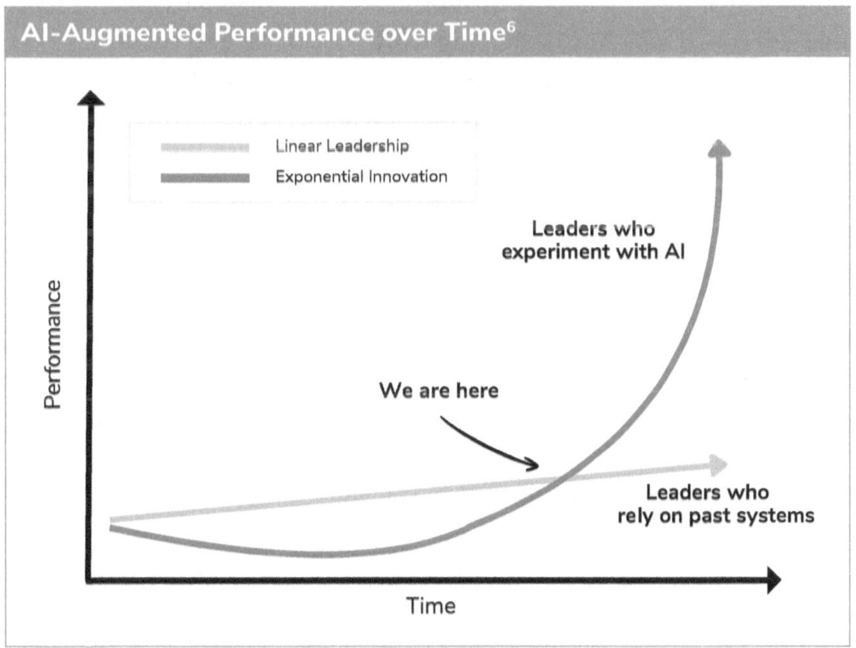

---

6. Diagram inspired by Singularity University Exponential Curve, https://www.su .org/resources/.

The market is not waiting for you.

- Between October 2025 and February 2026, Amazon cut 30,000 middle-management jobs[7].
- In 2025, Meta paid over $300 million to attract top AI talent[8].
- In early 2026, candidates with AI-related skills commanded a 23% wage premium, significantly higher than the premium for a master's degree (13%) or a bachelor's degree (8%).
- 32% of Gen Z workers report being "extremely worried" about job obsolescence, the highest of any demographic.[9]

Talent is reorganizing around this curve at a blistering pace.

In January 2026, the Burning Glass Institute[10] analyzed millions of job postings before and after the release of ChatGPT. Their findings offer some of the first empirical evidence—not projections, but measurable shifts—of how AI is reshaping work.

The skills most vulnerable to automation were **16% more likely to decline** in demand, while AI-augmented skills were **7% more likely to increase**.

The labor market isn't collapsing. It's rebalancing. But here's the part most leaders miss: Across **759 occupations**, automation exposure and augmentation exposure are **strongly positively correlated (r = 0.87)**. That means the roles most vulnerable to automation are the same roles being augmented the most. This shift isn't centered on manual labor. It's concentrated in knowledge work.

AI isn't neatly sorting the workforce into "safe" and "at risk." It's redesigning knowledge work from within. The project manager whose scheduling tasks are automated is the same project manager whose

---

7. Palmer, Annie. "Amazon to Cut Management Layers, End Remote Work in Productivity Push." CNBC, September 16, 2024.

8. Heath, Alex. "The AI Talent War: Why Meta is Spending Hundreds of Millions to Keep Engineers." The Verge, November 14, 2025.

9. Puntoni, Stefano, Prasanna Tambe, and Jeremy Korst. Accountable Acceleration: Gen AI Fast-Tracks Into the Enterprise. Philadelphia: Wharton Human-AI Research and GBK Collective, October 2025.

10. Burning Glass Institute, Beyond the Binary: How Automation and Augmentation Are Combining to Reshape Work, January 2026.

strategic responsibilities expand. The financial analyst who no longer builds models from scratch is the same analyst who now interprets, challenges, and pressure tests AI-generated output.

The unit of change isn't the job. It's the judgment required for the job. And judgment is exactly where advantage now compounds. Jensen Huang, CEO of NVIDIA, put it perfectly: **"AI won't take your job. But someone who can use it will."**

Case Study: Role Modeling Learning
Joe Noreña, former COO at HSBC

Joe Noreña, former COO of Global Markets Americas at HSBC, didn't treat learning as a task to be delegated or scheduled once a year. He embedded it directly into how he worked.

When new graduates joined the organization, Joe would sit with them and bring real problems he was actively working on—not as tests but as learning sessions. He wanted to see **how they approached the problem**, what tools they reached for, and how their thinking differed from his own.

Junior hires introduced novel techniques, new tools, and alternative ways of framing the challenge. In a highly hierarchical organization like HSBC, this behavior sent a powerful signal. When one of the most senior leaders learns openly from the most junior team members, hierarchy collapses where it matters most: **learning speed**.

This is exactly the kind of behavior the AI era requires. By learning in the open, Joe made experimentation safe for everyone else. Teams didn't wait for permission. They learned faster because learning had been legitimized at the top. That's leadership.

The New Leadership Divide

What is most important isn't who knows the answer, but who knows how to get the answer, from where, fastest.

This is no longer a philosophical debate. It's an operating system divide.

In every organization, there are now only two types of leaders: those who experiment and learn publicly with AI and those who rely on legacy systems.

Leaders Who Experiment with AI	Leaders Who Rely on Legacy Systems
Capture work as data	Rely on memory
Synthesize automatically	Rebuild context manually
Test assumptions continuously	Defend past decisions
Collapse decision cycles	Wait for dashboards
Prepare before meetings	Reconstruct during meetings
Enter conversations with clarity	Catch up in conversations
Increase judgment work	Stay busy with execution
Reduce coordination overhead	Add layers of approval
Push decisions to the edge	Pull decisions up the hierarchy
Learn publicly	Learn privately (or not at all)
Adapt daily	Rely on past success
Compound advantage	Accumulate friction

The gap between these groups is compounding daily, and it does not close on its own. Beginning your learning journey with AI is the only way forward.

Where to Start

In the face of the AI disruption taking over the market, 88% of companies have defaulted to "AI transformation" as their top priority, according to McKinsey[11].

AI task forces, centers of excellence, and massive global rollouts are the wrong starting points. They're too big, too slow, and too inefficient.

The right place to begin is with you.

---

11. McKinsey & Company. The State of AI: How Organizations Are Rewiring to Capture Value. McKinsey Global Survey, March 12, 2025.

When you experiment with these new technologies, you learn. When you share what you're trying, discovering, or failing with, you are role modeling. When you integrate AI into your workflow, your team follows. When teams follow, the organization shifts.

Artificial organizations emerge not through mandates and massive transformation initiatives, but through leaders who choose to practice the new behaviors in the open, not preach them.

Urgency doesn't have to create fear. If anything, this moment should spark excitement. Because once you start working this way, you won't want to go back—and that is where transformation becomes personal.

CHAPTER 2

UNLEARN TO LEAD: TRAITS BEFORE TOOLS

When you start with who you are and how you do your best work, everything else becomes simpler and more scalable.

When I started writing *Unlearn*[1] in 2017, I did what I had always done: I sat down and typed. It was painful. Every sentence felt heavy. Every typo broke momentum. Being dyslexic meant progress was slow and frustrating, and the harder I pushed, the worse it got.

I told myself this was normal. Real writers type. They grind. They pour blood, sweat, and tears into their books. They sit by roaring fires, drinking red wine in purple velvet jackets and turn out pages for hours. I tried the wine and jacket. Those didn't work either.

I'd written *Lean Enterprise* as part of a team. Maybe I wasn't actually capable of doing this on my own? The identity I'd built—someone who executes, who gets stuff done—was suddenly working against me.

I stopped and asked a different question: **How do I actually do my best work?**

Not how I was taught to work, not how it looks from the outside, but how I know I do my best work.

The answer wasn't typing. It was talking.

---

1. Barry O'Reilly, *Unlearn: Let Go of Past Success to Achieve Extraordinary Results* (New York: McGraw-Hill Education, 2018).

I think out loud. I sharpen ideas in conversation. Momentum comes when I can explore, question, and push back in real time.

Once I realized that, everything changed. Instead of forcing myself into a workflow that didn't suit me, I redesigned the work according to how I actually get into flow.

I hired a writer, Peter, to interview me. I'd bullet-point the shape of each chapter, and then we'd jump on a call and talk it through from beginning to end. He'd ask questions, push back on ideas, and sharpen my thinking.

We'd record the conversation, run it through an AI transcription tool, and generate the output before we'd even hung up. Peter would take that raw transcript, shape it, refine the language, and send it back as our minimum viable chapter. We went from *ideating to iterating* in hours.

Each conversation felt productive. Each draft felt alive. And for the first time, the words sounded like *me*.

That's when it clicked. My natural *trait* was speaking to communicate ideas. My highest-leverage *task* was generating content. The right *tool* didn't replace that; it *accelerated* it. I didn't need to be a writer who typed. I needed to be a writer who created content.

Conversations became drafts. Drafts became artifacts. AI handled the friction in between.

The breakthrough wasn't technological. It was personal. I didn't become a better writer because of a tool. I became a better writer because I stopped pretending that I worked like someone else. That was my unlearning moment.

The Shift Isn't About AI. It's About You.

This is where most leaders get stuck. They think AI adoption starts with tools. It doesn't. It starts with **honesty**.

Honesty about:

* how you think

* where you add value

* what strains your judgment

* which parts of your work no longer deserve your attention

AI doesn't force this reckoning. It *reveals* it.

That's why this moment feels uncomfortable for so many leaders. Not because the technology is threatening your relevance but because it exposes the gap between how you work and how you *could* work. Unlearning is the act of closing that gap.

Traits Before Tools

Every leader has natural traits, patterns for how they create, process, and make sense of information.

Different leaders perform best by being:

- **verbal**: talking, debating, questioning out loud, storytelling
- **visual**: writing, sketching, diagramming
- **receptive**: listening, reading, observing
- **physical**: walking, prototyping
- **analytical**: contemplating, problem-solving, facilitating, role-playing

These traits aren't preferences. They're your unique leverage.

Most leaders never design their work around them. Instead, they inherit workflows that reward endurance, responsiveness, and visibility.

AI flips that equation. When machines handle administration such as capture, recall, and synthesis, **your value concentrates around judgment**. And judgment is the scarcest resource in high-performance leadership.

This means that the work that matters most now is:

- framing the right problems
- making good decisions during uncertainty
- showing up and being present when the stakes are high

That work cannot be automated. That work is uniquely human. And it *can* be amplified, if you stop fighting how you naturally operate.

The Trait–Task–Tool (3T) Model

When beginning to explore AI, most leaders start with tools. That's the mistake. Tools are the last piece of the system. The order matters:

Traits → Tasks → Tools

This isn't productivity sequencing. It's judgment infrastructure design.

When you start with *who* you are and *how* you do your best work, everything else becomes simpler and more scalable.

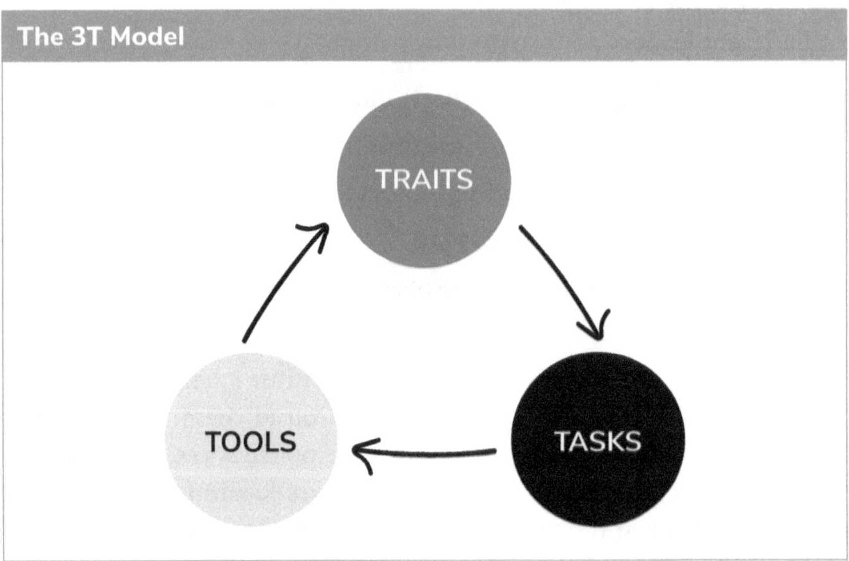

Traits: How You Naturally Work

When it comes to AI, most people never stop to examine their traits, yet it's your natural behavior, preferences, and information patterns that determine everything.

You already have ways of:

- creating information (writing, drawing, talking, thinking out loud)

- capturing it (notes, slides, recordings, memory)

- leveraging it (dashboards, summaries, messaging)

- reusing it (pattern recognition, strategy)
- recalling it (informing decisions, sense-checking)

Most leaders only do the first two. AI unlocks the other three, but only if you know your natural starting point.

For example, when Peter and I were working on *Unlearn*, I realized that writing slowed me down. I'm dyslexic, so the keyboard was a bottleneck. My natural trait, talking, was my superpower. So we redesigned our workflow: *talk → transcribe → edit → iterate → complete.*

It felt like cheating because of how fast we moved. This is the power of optimizing your traits.

Tasks: How You Get Leverage

Follow this simple rule: **Automate the repeatable. Amplify the creative.**

Every leader's tasks fall into two buckets:

High-Leverage Tasks	(Necessary) Time-Suck Tasks
preparation	typing notes
synthesis	writing follow-ups
strategic thinking	reformatting updates
judgment	hunting for documents
coaching	remembering context
design	preparing decks
decisions	sharing information for alignment and future use

AI is built for the necessary, time-suck tasks. You are built for high-leverage tasks. When you automate time-suck administration, you create space for the work only you can do.

For me, this changed everything. By automating my 1:1 coaching routines (*preparation → presence → follow-up*), I went from four coaching calls a day to seven, with higher NPS, deeper insights, and zero burnout. We also got to decision points sooner, so meetings ran shorter, giving me more time back. I wasn't working harder. Automation enabled me to work in a full flow state on the highest-priority tasks while limiting the time-sucking parts of the job I was doing.

Tools: The Last Step, Not the First

Tools matter but only after you know:

- your natural traits (how you work)
- your highest-leverage tasks (where you create value)

When you align your traits and your tasks, you reduce cognitive friction, judgment sharpens, and tools become multipliers.

Start with traits. Follow with tasks. Then choose tools.

Start Small: Meetings as the First Domino

Meetings are one of the poorest uses of time, money, and human capacity. Leaders are now spending nearly 23 hours a week sitting in meetings, double what it was in the 1960s[2]. Even then, only 35% bother to show up with an agenda, and just 22% end with a clear outcome. Sixty-seven percent of meetings are rated ineffective or a poor use of time[3]. It's no surprise the US loses $37 billion a year on unproductive meetings alone[4].

Meetings are not communication rituals. They are decision engines, and most are leaking value.

When I asked myself honest questions about how I worked, I realized I spent most of my time in meetings—many of them virtual—talking, problem-solving, and making decisions. The real burden wasn't the meeting itself. It was all the preparation, the capturing, the synthesizing, the sharing of the information afterward, and the tracking of outcomes.

My first step with machine augmentation was obvious. I started experimenting with an AI-powered meeting assistant that could capture everything that was said and create an audit trail—a database and digital asset I could refer to at any point in the future—that allowed

---

2. Leslie A. Perlow, Constance Noonan Hadley, and Eunice Eun, "Stop the Meeting Madness," Harvard Business School (July–August 2017).

3. Work Meetings in Numbers: Latest Meeting Statistics [2025]. ArchieApp Blog, 2026.

4. Mark Elias, "Time Wasted in Meetings: 39 Meeting Statistics," Discovery ABA (March 26, 2025).

me to be in the moment—fully present with people—because I wasn't worried about missing anything.

That single experiment was an epiphany. It made me realize that meetings were my key moment of leadership, where creative problem-solving happened, decisions were made, and progress was forged.

The best leaders in the world have high decision velocity and decision advantage: speed to decide and the quality of insight to support them in the room when making tough choices. With the right support, you could be one of them, someone who shows up highly prepared, stands out, and creates a better experience for everyone. A leader who makes better decisions with greater clarity, confidence, and conviction.

The Beginning of Your Transformation

Remember, artificial organizations aren't designed around tools. They're designed by **leaders who understand themselves deeply enough to work differently.**

This was further underlined by Wharton's 2025 Enterprise AI Adoption Report,[5] which found that, although **AI deployment surged 400%** across enterprises in 2024–2025, **ROI remains concentrated in 12-18% of companies**—those that *treat AI as a transformation, not a tool.*

You don't start by installing AI. You start by installing a new operating system for yourself.

You must understand your identity, so your behaviors can shift, and your leadership can transform.

Identity → Behavior → Transformation

Traits before tasks. Tasks before tools. Tools before outcomes.

These outcomes renew your traits as you become stronger, clearer, and more confident than before.

---

5. Wharton Human-AI Research and GBK Collective, 2025 AI Adoption Report: Gen AI Fast-Tracks Into the Enterprise, Knowledge at Wharton (October 28, 2025), https://knowledge.wharton.upenn.edu/special-report/2025-ai-adoption-report/.

The One Step That Changes Everything

If you do nothing else after this chapter, do this: **capture your work as data.** One meeting, one conversation, one reflection at the end of the day—not perfectly, not publicly, just intentionally.

Once your work becomes something you can see, search, and synthesize—an asset you can return to—your thinking begins to compound. Preparation stops being exhausting. Decisions stop feeling rushed. Presence returns.

Leaders who experiment personally move faster than organizations that launch massive initiatives because unlearning doesn't spread through policy. It spreads through behavior—and you have the opportunity to role model it, lead it, and stand out in your company, the workforce, and the market.

PART II

STRENGTHEN JUDGMENT UNDER PRESSURE

"Clarity before you enter the room determines authority inside it."

Pressure does not break judgment. It reveals whether structure exists. When synthesis is rushed, decision latency increases, options narrow, and authority weakens.

In this part, you apply Traits–Tasks–Tools (3T) to redirect attention toward high-leverage judgment. You use Capture–Transcribe–Synthesize–Act (CTSA) and structured prompting to reduce cognitive drag before critical moments. Preparation becomes deliberate. Options are shaped before stakes rise. Presence strengthens because thinking is disciplined, not improvised.

Judgment under pressure is not instinct. It is designed.

CHAPTER 3

TURN EVERY INTERACTION INTO AN ASSET

Less admin; more clarity. Collapse decision latency.

always thought productivity was about discipline: clearer notes, better systems, tighter calendars. I was wrong.

The real shift came when I stopped treating meetings, conversations, and fleeting thoughts as *moments* and started treating them as **information assets.**

Every minute you spend talking, listening, or deciding something important is generating a signal. Most leaders let that signal evaporate, not because they're careless, but because the tools we grew up with were never designed to capture thinking at executive speed. AI changes that.

This chapter is about one simple idea: **Every interaction is an information asset—if you capture it properly.**

It's not meant to replace your judgment or automate your leadership but to amplify what you already do best.

Human + Machine = Better Outcomes

Better outcomes don't come from humans or machines in isolation. They come from **human judgment deliberately paired with machine intelligence.**

Let's be clear about the traps on both sides.

Human-only leadership got you here. Your instincts, experience, and pattern recognition built your career. Maybe it even took you to the top. But the game has changed. You're no longer competing against people who rely on instinct alone. You're competing against leaders who combine human *and* machine intelligence—people who can recall conversations with precision, spot patterns across months of meetings, and prepare in minutes instead of hours. Instinct alone is no longer enough.

At the other extreme is **machine-only leadership**, where leaders delegate thinking to AI, trust outputs blindly, and let tools make decisions without human judgment in the loop. That path leads to sloppy outcomes, reputational risk, and real consequences.

We've already seen this play out. In 2025, Deloitte admitted to using generative AI (GPT-4o) to produce a report[1] for the Australian government that contained fabricated citations and other errors. As a result, Deloitte agreed to refund the final installment of its AU$440,000 contract with the Department of Employment and Workplace Relations (DEWR), after the client had to correct the flawed report.

That example—and many like it—reminds us of something important: The answer is not human *or* machine. It's **human + machine = better outcomes**.

Recent field research from Harvard[2] makes this visible in the data. Studying hundreds of professionals grappling with real innovation challenges within Procter & Gamble, the researchers found that individuals working with AI performed as well as human teams working without it—a clear signal that machine intelligence can replicate many of the benefits leaders once depended on human collaboration to provide. More importantly, **when human judgment and AI were deliberately paired, the likelihood of producing top-quality outcomes nearly tripled.**

---

1. Craig Hale, "Deloitte Forced to Refund Aussie Government After Admitting It Used AI to Produce Error-Strewn Report," TechRadar, October 7, 2025, https://www .techradar.com/pro/deloitte-forced-to-refund-aussie-government-after-admitting-it -used-ai-to-produce-error-strewn-report.

2. Fabrizio Dell'Acqua et al., "The Cybernetic Teammate: A Field Experiment on Generative AI Reshaping Teamwork and Expertise," Harvard Business School Working Paper, No. 25-043, March 2025, Faculty & Research, Harvard Business School, accessed February 18, 2026, https://www.hbs.edu/faculty/Pages/item.aspx ?num=67197.

The mechanism wasn't blind automation. AI improved recall, expanded the option set, and reduced cognitive load—sharpening human judgment and decision-making. AI didn't replace thinking. It improved it.

That's the leadership shift this book will help you make. Your judgment plus machine recall. Your intuition plus machine synthesis. Your presence plus machine precision.

The result? Better outcomes.

Why Presence Is Now a Leadership Advantage

Here's the paradox I see with senior leaders: You spend most of your day in conversations that matter, yet you're rarely fully present for them because your brain is too busy:

- taking notes
- remembering action items
- worrying you'll forget something
- preparing the follow-up
- replaying the last meeting while you're still in this one

When you can let go of that mental overhead and *trust* that information is being captured accurately, something changes. You listen differently. You ask better questions. You notice tone, hesitation, and energy shifts.

When cognitive overhead drops, executive presence rises and decision quality improves.

AI doesn't make you less personal in meetings. It enables you to be **more present, more human.**

A Breakthrough

My real performance breakthrough happened in a **high-stakes board meeting.** You know the kind: ideas flying, smart people building on each other's ideas, sharp challenges, half-formed insights becoming clear in real time. The room had energy—momentum—that sense that something important was taking shape.

Then the meeting ended. A few hours later, the minutes arrived. Technically correct; strategically useless. They captured what was said, but none of **what mattered**. The language we used to describe the customer, the tension around trade-offs, the moment when someone reframed the problem and everyone leaned in—all gone. No clear ownership. No explicit measures of progress. No shared understanding of what "great" actually looked like. The magic of the moment evaporated.

A month later, we reconvened. We spent the first twenty minutes trying to remember:

- What did we actually agree?
- Who was meant to lead this?
- How far did we get?

Everyone had been in the same room, but we each had a different memory of the event.

That's when it hit me: We weren't failing at creation. We were failing at **capture**—not capture as documentation, but as the first step in building judgment infrastructure. We were generating incredibly valuable information and letting it disappear. That's the cost of treating meetings as moments instead of assets.

Once I saw that, I couldn't unsee it. Meetings weren't interruptions. They were **high-value data-generation sessions**. And if I captured them properly—at full fidelity—we could:

- recall conversations with precision
- preserve intent, not just outcomes
- follow up with clarity and accountability
- track progress over time instead of relying on memory
- continuously build context to be recalled, reused, and leveraged to train all future ventures
- use every session to learn, improve, and compound decision velocity and decision advantage

That insight became the foundation of my personal AI operating system. I never went back.

Your Core Executive Routine

Every leader needs a first workflow. Not a complex system. Not ten tools. Just one simple learning loop.

Mine is **CTSA: Capture → Transcribe → Synthesize → Act**

It's how you fuel decision velocity and decision advantage, the twin engines of AI-augmented leadership.

Think of it as the human-plus-machine evolution of PDCA—Plan, Do, Check, Act—popularized by W. Edwards Deming in the 1950s yet reimagined for today's leaders working with AI to accelerate learning and compound improvement.

PDCA worked because it treated work as an experiment, not a one-off decision. Each loop tightened feedback, reduced waste, and improved outcomes. What's changed today is **speed**. AI collapses the distance between doing the work and learning from it. Leaders can now run this loop continuously—not quarterly—with terabytes of information they capture.

As Secil Tabli Watson, NACD Board Member; Former EVP & Head of Digital for Commercial Banking, Wells Fargo shared, "This approach changed how I prepare, how I decide, and how I show up in the boardroom."

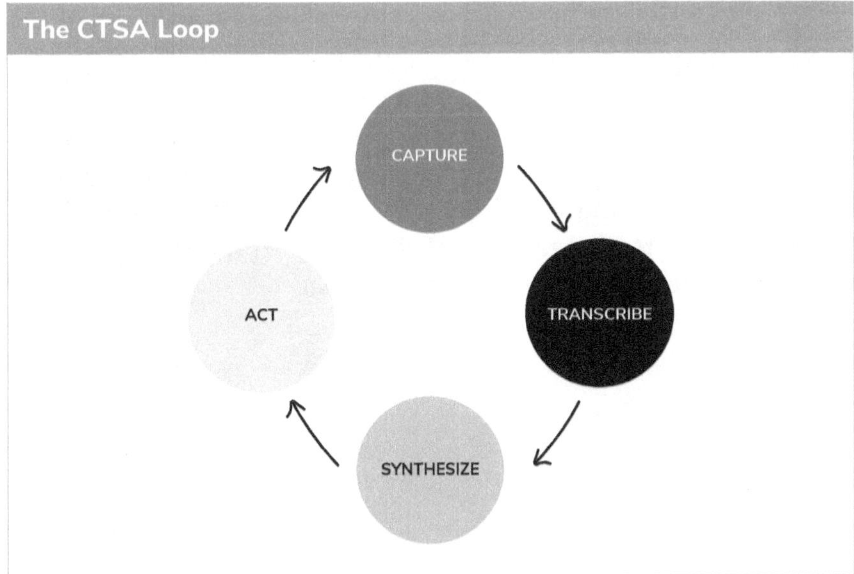

CTSA is PDCA for executive-plus-machine work in the age of intelligence:

- **Capture** the interaction.
- **Transcribe** it automatically.
- **Synthesize** meaning, patterns, and intent.
- **Act** with clarity.

Do this consistently, and the outcomes from every interaction compound.

What This Looks Like in Practice

After a one-hour coaching session, I can send a thoughtful follow-up email with clear, hyper personalized insight and an asset in under a minute. It includes:

- key themes
- concerns and opportunities
- direct quotes that capture intent
- agreed actions
- focus for next time

People often ask how I can be so present *and* so fast.

Once you start doing this systematically for meetings, one-on-ones, weekly reviews, and strategy sessions, something powerful happens. Your work becomes an asset. Your thinking becomes traceable. You stop relying on memory and start relying on evidence. You don't use AI just for productivity. You leverage it for **better judgment, better outcomes, and better experiences** for the people you lead.

Capture Everything (Decide Later)

Most leaders under-capture. They wait to decide what matters *before* recording. That's backward.

Capture first. Decide later. You can't synthesize what you never recorded. When capture is cheap, recall becomes infinite.

- Use an AI Meeting Assistant, such as Microsoft Copilot, Fireflies.ai, or Otter.ai for *Capture* and *Transcribe*.
- Leverage Large Learning Models (LLMs), such as OpenAI's GPT, Anthropic's Claude, or Google's Gemini for *Synthesize*.
- *Act* is reserved for humans. You must own it.

This isn't about tools. It's about flow.

If your work disappears at the end of the week, your advantage disappears with it.

Exercise: Interactions into Assets

Don't overhaul everything. Start small. Start personal.

Step 1: Pick One Interaction

What's one recurring meeting or critical conversation that matters most if you get it right?

Step 2: Capture and Transcribe It

Record it or record your thoughts immediately after. Transcribe the information into a file—Word document, Google Doc, or PDF—an asset you can save.

Step 3: Synthesize

Upload it into an LLM, and ask:

- What actually mattered here?
- What decisions were made?
- What questions remain open?

Step 4: Act

Ask the LLM to help you:

- Send the follow-up.
- Set the actions.
- Prepare differently next time.

That's it. Less admin; more clarity. Collapse decision latency.

From Capture and Transcribe to Synthesize

Once every interaction becomes an asset, a new problem emerges. You're no longer short on information; you're surrounded by it.

How do you turn captured signals into confident decisions faster than everyone else?

With the power of prompts.

CHAPTER 4

DO YOUR BEST RESEARCH AND DECISION-MAKING

AI doesn't replace judgment; it sharpens it.
A leader's edge isn't information; it's interpretation.

Today, you can capture almost everything. You can talk, type, draw, diagram, even take pictures, and a machine will record it. Meetings are transcribed. Calls are logged. Documents are searchable. Dashboards multiply by the quarter. Yet decision-making feels slower.

The problem isn't data. It's synthesis—and judgment collapses when synthesis is slow.

Most leaders fall short on:

- **signal**—knowing the information is relevant, reliable, and sufficient
- **convergence**—integrating inputs into a coherent view
- **composure**—maintaining decision space under pressure
- **commitment**—deciding without rework or second-guessing

Organizations are trained to produce more inputs, not better judgment. AI changes this, but only if you stop using it to gather more data and produce sloppy output.

You need to start using human and machine intelligence to do your best research, pressure test judgment, explore strategies and scenarios, and decide with clarity and confidence under uncertainty.

What Leaders Are Really Struggling With

Across coaching conversations with CEOs, C-suite executives, and senior leaders, the same research and decision-making friction shows up again and again:

- **data overload**—too many dashboards, not enough meaning
- **slow signal detection**—patterns surface too late or are hard to spot
- **fragmented information**—meetings, documents, and metrics don't connect
- **latency from Individual Contributors (ICs) to leaders**—insight takes weeks to travel
- **weak synthesis to decisions**—lots of activity, little resolution

None of these challenges are new, and they aren't caused by a lack of data capture. They're caused by **leaders not being clear about what they're actually trying to decide.** AI doesn't magically fix that. It can collapse cycle time, surface patterns, and pressure test instincts but only when leaders are clear about the decision in front of them.

Most leaders use AI to retrieve information, as if it were a search engine, instead of leveraging it to **frame the problem, challenge assumptions, and decide.** The result is more output and quicker not better judgment.

That's the difference between more information and greater synthesis, between activity and action, and between faster output and better outcomes.

Case Study: Connecting the Dots
Steve Elliott, Founder and CEO of Dotwork

No matter how much is invested in project management tools, process design, and team working agreements, why do executives keep using spreadsheets to track decisions?

Steve Elliott has spent more than two decades as an executive with decision-making power. He's a serial entrepreneur with four exits, former Head of Product at Atlassian (after selling AgileCraft, now Jira Align, to the company), and author of *The Decisive Company*. He's worked with leadership teams across organizations of every size and seen the same pattern repeat.

When decisions matter most, **leaders stop trusting systems and start building spreadsheets**—not because spreadsheets are good but because they're the only tool leaders feel is flexible enough to *think with.* That's the signal.

The Hidden Truth: Decisions Don't Fail Because of Bad Data

In Steve's experience, executives rarely struggle with access to information. They struggle with **synthesis.**

- Signals are scattered across teams and tools.

- Narratives conflict by function.

- Historical context disappears every time priorities shift.

- Leaders pay a heavy cognitive tax just rebuilding understanding.

In response, leaders do something rational but inefficient. They manually connect the dots. That's where decision latency creeps in.

The Breakthrough Insight: Decisions Have a Repeatable Shape

Over years of working with leadership teams, Steve identified a crucial pattern: Although inputs change, the decision shape remains the same.

Most strategic decisions boil down to the same questions:

- What's happening right now?

- What's changed since last time?

- Where are signals converging or diverging?

- What assumptions are we making?

- What happens if we're wrong?

The failure wasn't tooling. It was that leaders had no fast, repeatable way to run this thinking loop under pressure. This is where AI comes in not as automation, but as **judgment infrastructure,** when leaders redesign how judgment flows.

Steve built Dotwork, a platform that connects the dots, enabling decisive action aligned to strategy.

How Leaders Can Be Decisive Today Without Enterprise Platforms

Any executive can start connecting the dots using tools they already have, such as ChatGPT, Copilot, Claude, and Gemini. Tools will evolve and capabilities will change, but disciplined decision-making requires clarity, assumption checking, challenge, and decisiveness.

The shift is simple but profound.

Treat AI as Judgment Infrastructure, Not a Search Engine

Use AI to do research, not gather data.

Instead of asking: "Summarize this."

Ask: "What decision is this information pointing toward?"

Paste what you already have:

- meeting notes

- metrics snapshots

- strategy documents

- email or Slack summaries

- customer support call transcripts and feedback

- diagrams, photos, charts

You're not looking for final answers. You're creating **context continuity.**

This is research, not retrieval.

Use AI as a Safe Space to Explore Half-Formed Ideas

One of the biggest hidden constraints on executives is this: Once you say something out loud, people treat it as a commitment. Or worse, start extrapolating doomsday scenarios that may never happen. That makes it risky to explore uncertainty in public.

AI gives you **private thinking space** to:

- test an idea before socializing it

- explore scenarios without signaling direction

- strengthen your thinking before inviting challenge

As one executive told me: "It's the first place I can be honest about what I don't know."

Chapter 5 will cover this at further length. For now, just notice what it gives you: space.

Pressure Test Judgment Before High-Stakes Moments

Before a board or executive meeting, ask AI to:

- argue against your preferred option
- surface disconfirming evidence
- explain where your logic might be weak
- list what would need to be true for you to be wrong

This isn't about being pessimistic. It's about **showing up decisive, not defensive.**

Over time, by inviting challenge and an alternative perspective and assumption checking, you're building decision resilience, not just speed.

Your human instincts interpret the machine insights to improve judgment, but how do you get quality insights?

The machine needs a prompt.

What Is a Prompt?

A prompt is not a clever question, a trick, or a measure of how "good" you are at AI.

A prompt is how you frame the problem for the machine.

Think of it like briefing a sharp chief of staff. If you're vague, you'll get something generic. If you're clear, you'll get something useful. If you ask it to be brutally honest with you, it will be.

Remember: the machine's default posture is to be helpful, which often means agreeing with you. Your job is to frame the problem so it can challenge your thinking, not reinforce it.

Used well, prompts allow AI to:

* synthesize across inputs you don't have time to reconcile
* pressure test your judgment
* explore strategies and scenarios safely
* help you decide with clarity and confidence under uncertainty

Better synthesis leads to stronger decisions.

How to Write the Perfect Prompt

Greg Brockman, OpenAI Co-Founder and President, shared a simple structure for writing better prompts[1], often referred to as the "o1 prompt" framework. It's not clever. It's not technical. It's how executives already think when they're clear. It has four parts: goal, output, warning, and context.

The o1 Prompt Framework

Field	Purpose
Goal	What you're trying to achieve—the desired end state or outcome. It should be action-oriented and clear.
Output	What specific deliverable or format you want (e.g., email, slide deck, blog post, roadmap, table, etc). Helps guide structure.
Warning	What to avoid—common pitfalls, tone issues, formatting errors, or domain-specific risks.
Context	Relevant background that helps the AI respond intelligently. Include people involved, business situation, tone expectations, constraints, etc.

---

1. Brockman, Greg (@gdb). "The first time in human history that a computer can perform any task a person can do with a computer is close." X, January 13, 2025, 9:22 p.m. https://x.com/gdb/status/1878489681702310392.

Goal

Write the goal like you're addressing a sharp chief of staff.

Not: "Analyze this data."

But: "Help me decide what to prioritize before a board meeting."

If the goal is vague, the output will be generic.

Output

Specify the format you want the information in.

Executives don't need essays. They need **usable artifacts**:

- a one-page decision brief

- a table ranking options by impact and risk

- bullets suitable for a board pre-read

If you don't specify the format, AI will choose one, and it's usually long.

Warnings

Control risk and failure modes with the following instructions:

- Don't hallucinate facts.

- Flag uncertainty explicitly.

- Avoid jargon.

- Include counterarguments.

- Ask clarifying questions if data is missing.

Do these to avoid the *happy path*, the common trap of assuming everything will go perfectly, which often masks hidden risks and critical errors.

AI produces convincing language, not verified truth. For meaningful decisions, confirm key facts independently and treat every response as a working draft, not a final answer.

Context

This includes:

- transcripts
- notes
- metrics
- strategy documents
- constraints
- stakeholder dynamics

Context only helps *after* the goal and output are clear. Otherwise, you've just given the machine a big pile of information.

Exercise: Executive Prompt

This is the structure I teach first because it works across a range of problems, teams, and tools. It forces you to be clear about what you're actually trying to decide.

Goal

- What I'm trying to achieve is: [**decision/insight/ recommendation**]
- *(If you can't state this clearly, don't move on yet.)*

Output

- Return the output, so I can actually use: [**brief/table/bullets/ memo**]
- Include sections: [**A, B, C**] *(substitute for perspectives you want addressed)*
- Write it for: [**board/executive team/leadership group**]

Warning

- Do not: [assume/hallucinate/over-generalize]
- If uncertain: [flag gaps and list what would help]
- Make sure to include: [risks, trade-offs, assumptions, counterarguments]

Context

- Here's the relevant background to work with: [paste transcripts, notes, metrics, documents]
- Focus on what matters for what I want to achieve, not everything that exists.

This four-part framework enables you to be clear about the decision you need to make before you ask AI for help.

For more prompts and templates, go to artificialorganizations.com to access the toolkit.

Use Disconfirming Questions

AI is optimized to be helpful, which often means agreeing with you. That's dangerous if you stop at the first output from your first input. Strong leaders interrogate the output, using disconfirming questions to strengthen their thinking:

General Research and Insight Generation

- "What assumptions are being made in this answer?" This helps you understand hidden logic or potential bias in the AI's synthesis.
- "What might be missing or not represented in this perspective?" This surfaces blind spots or ignored stakeholders/data.
- "Can you outline 3 key points to support each option for a board-level audience?" This refines clarity and executive alignment.

Strategic Exploration and Market Testing

- "If we pursued this idea, what would the first 5 questions from a skeptical customer be?" This is great for customer-centric thinking and pressure testing.

- "What are the leading indicators we should watch to validate this direction early?" This is useful for experimentation and test/learn strategies.

- "If this idea fails, what are the most likely reasons why?" This promotes pre-mortem thinking and stronger risk strategy.

Start a Prompt Library

Most leaders treat prompts as disposable. They ask a question. They get an answer. They move on. That's fine at the beginning. But it's not how leverage is built.

A Prompt Library is how you turn good questions into repeatable decision assets that you can use over time across different activities: preparing for board meetings, prioritizing competing initiatives, making sense of fragmented inputs, pressure testing strategies, getting ready for a hard conversation, deciding what not to do. The **shape of the decision repeats**, even if the data and contexts change. A Prompt Library captures that shape.

Over time, your Prompt Library becomes:

- a record of how you think at your best

- a shortcut back to clarity under pressure

- a way to avoid reinventing your decision process every time

In this sense, prompts are not technical instructions. They are structured judgment.

If a prompt helps you make a better decision more than once, save it. That's how leverage compounds.

Keep it personal at first, and then socialize it with your team later.

As Steve Elliot, CEO of Dotwork shared, "Leaders don't lack data; they lack a fast, repeatable system for thinking clearly under pressure." Your Prompt Library can be a go-to resource in those moments.

Exercise: Design a Simple AI Research and Decision Routine

Start small. Make it real.

Step 1. Identify 2–3 decisions you regularly struggle with.

Step 2. List what frustrates you today:

- slow answers
- conflicting inputs
- weak synthesis

Step 3. Use the Goal–Output–Warnings–Context framework on one live decision.

Step 4. Pressure test your thinking with disconfirming questions.

Step 5. Save what worked. Start a simple Prompt Library.

Five Questions to Get Started

1. Where do I consistently feel under-prepared before decisions?
2. What signals do I wish surfaced sooner?
3. What meetings would improve if I arrived pre-synthesized?
4. Where am I mistaking volume for clarity?
5. What decisions deserve a reusable prompt?

Never Outsource Your Thinking

One CEO I work with asked an underperforming employee to create a personal development plan. The employee returned with a polished, AI-generated document. It was excellent, but it wasn't theirs.

When asked whether they had written it—and whether they would commit to it—the truth surfaced. It was not their plan. It was a machine's plan, and the employee opted out of following through with it. Trust was lost. The employee exited the company, which was the right outcome.

AI accelerates thinking. It does not replace ownership.

The Next Level

Different tools are designed for different kinds of work. **Leaders get leverage by aligning the task and tool to their traits,** not by using one tool for everything.

- Best for strategic Q&A, synthesis, reframing, and decision preparation: ChatGPT Pro, Claude, Microsoft Copilot
- Best for fast, cited research when external validation matters: Perplexity, Elicit, Consensus
- Best for accelerating insight in recurring decision contexts: Custom prompts; custom GPTs/Copilot Agents; prompt templates stored in Notion, Google Docs, or internal wikis

The power move isn't the tool. It's the prompt discipline.

The leverage isn't in using more tools. It's in knowing **which tool sharpens judgment for the task at hand.** This only improves with experimentation, experience, and practice.

Note: We cover tools in greater detail in Chapter 7: Your AI Tool Stack, with more information available at artificialorganizations.com.

What Improvement Looks Like

Here are performance improvements Steve Elliott describes seeing when organizations adopt AI-assisted research and decision-making—whether via platforms like Dotwork or the disciplined use of AI tools.

- **Decision velocity: 30–50% reduction in time** from issue surfaced → decision made
- **Decision frequency: 2–3× increase** in meaningful decisions per quarter
- **Decision preparation time: 40–60% reduction** in executive prep time
- **Decision quality signals: higher follow-through rates,** fewer reversals, clearer trade-offs and risks
- **Organizational clarity: faster alignment** after decisions, fewer wait-and-see behaviors downstream

The biggest gain isn't speed alone. It's confidence during uncertainty.

AI doesn't make leaders decisive. It removes the friction that keeps them indecisive.

This becomes even more critical if your competitors are shortening their decision cycles more than you are. Incremental improvement won't be enough to close the gap created by structural divergence.

CHAPTER 5

USE AI AS A
THINKING PARTNER

Most leaders come to AI to boost productivity.
They stay because it gives them room to think.

Leaders lack space: to think clearly, to capture and explore half-formed ideas, to pressure test instincts before they harden into decisions that impact people, capital, and reputations.

As responsibilities increase, organizations scale, and environments accelerate, that space silently disappears. Decisions get heavier. Stakes rise. Visibility increases. The room to think—especially out loud—shrinks. Ideas that once benefited from debate now feel risky to share too early. Teams extrapolate. Rumors start. People assume intent where there is only exploration. So leaders do what they've always done when the system stops supporting them: they carry it alone. This benefits no one.

AI's promise isn't to make leaders smarter. It's to restore the thinking space that the ever-increasing pressures of leadership have erased. When leaders lose the space to think, decision quality declines long before performance metrics do.

The Invisible Problem

In hundreds of coaching sessions with CEOs, C-suite leaders, and senior operators, one pattern shows up again and again. Their best thinking doesn't happen in strategy offsites or innovation workshops.

59

It happens:

- walking between meetings
- driving home
- speaking with customers
- decompressing after a tough conversation
- during a "Eureka!" moment in the shower

These are micro-moments when the brain finally relaxes enough for intuition to surface. Yet most of that thinking is never captured in a system.

Leaders tell me:

- "I get good ideas, but I don't record them."
- "I don't have time to shape them into anything usable."
- "If I bring these half-baked thoughts to my team, people overreact."
- "I need challenge, but I struggle to find candid feedback."

This is the quiet tax of senior leadership: the absence of a safe, judgment-free space to think. Without that space, leaders either delay decisions or make them with less confidence than they should because they're cognitively overloaded.

The Reframe: AI Isn't a Tool. It's a Space to Think

Most executives approach AI through the lens of productivity:

- more research
- quicker summaries
- fewer hours spent preparing

Those gains matter, but they're table stakes. The real shift happens when leaders stop asking, How can AI help me work faster? and start asking, How can AI help me *think better*?

Used well, AI gives leaders something they've been missing for years: **a private, safe space to think.**

A place where you can:

- explore an idea without committing to it
- challenge your own assumptions before others do
- pressure test strategy without triggering fear or speculation
- kill weak ideas quickly and move on

Leaders who create these spaces for themselves accelerate faster because they understand that **AI doesn't replace judgment. It creates the conditions for better judgment.**

A Quick Anti-Pattern Check

Before going further, it's worth identifying three traps executives fall into:

- **Using AI as a smarter search engine.** Faster answers don't improve judgment.
- **Collecting prompts without changing behavior.** Insight without practice doesn't compound.
- **Delegating thinking instead of sharpening it.** If AI is deciding for you, you're weakening the very muscle you're paid to use.

Executives who avoid these traps don't use AI more. They use it more deliberately.

Core Behavior: Idea Capture

The most powerful behavior I see leaders adopt is deceptively simple. Instead of letting ideas get stuck in their head—lost, looping, or turning into cognitive load—they capture them deliberately, consistently, and privately in:

- voice notes
- messy bullets
- half-written paragraphs
- post-its, diagrams and sketches
- fragments from tough meetings

Then they use AI to organize, challenge, and refine that thinking.

Case Study: Talking It Out
Misty Shafer Sterne, VP at American Airlines

Misty Shafer Sterne is the Vice President of Commercial Technology at American Airlines, the world's largest airline. She regularly tests her thinking by talking it out with colleagues, customers, and partners to help improve her ideas. Inspired by Brené Brown's fantastic work and book *Dare to Lead*, she loves to "rumble."

A "rumble" is defined as a discussion, conversation, or meeting, where participants commit to leaning into vulnerability, staying curious, and being fearless in owning their parts. It is a deliberate, brave approach to addressing difficult, messy, or uncomfortable issues without knowing the exact outcome in advance.

Misty recognizes her best thinking doesn't always happen in strategy sessions. Her best ideas often come while she's moving–walking through an airport terminal or driving home—or in quiet moments between meetings.

Talking it out is her natural *trait* and a true talent. Once she started capturing voice notes and running them through AI, her thinking became a multiplier. She:

- shaped new geo-location operating models
- developed revenue ideas
- captured performance feedback for her team
- refined strategies far faster than before

At the same time, she noticed clear benefits:

- ideas stopped getting lost
- strategy work happened in micro-moments
- intuition turned into structured plans
- preparation time dropped dramatically

She didn't find more hours. She found leverage in small fractions of time compounded throughout her day.

Her ability to capture raw thoughts; process, improve, and bring them back to her team at high quality; or discard them quickly if they didn't hold up changed how she worked.

Misty's AI-Augmented Results

Area of Impact	What Changed	Metrics	Why This Matters
Geo-location operating models	Ideas moved faster from intuition to structured options	• Number of geo-specific operating models explored • Time from raw idea to stakeholder-ready model • Number of strategic options considered per geography	Increased strategic optionality and reduced time-to-clarity before decisions
Revenue idea development	Revenue thinking became more systematic and testable	• Volume of revenue concepts captured • Percentage translated into business cases or experiments • Time from idea capture to decision memo • Variety of revenue models explored	Improved discipline in revenue exploration without overcommitting resources
Team performance feedback	Feedback was captured closer to the moment and with higher fidelity	• Frequency of feedback captured after key interactions • Time between observation and documented feedback • Specificity of feedback (examples, behaviors, context) • Leader confidence in feedback conversations	Higher-quality coaching and clearer performance conversations

(continued)

Misty's AI-Augmented Results (continued)

Area of Impact	What Changed	Metrics	Why This Matters
Strategy refinement speed	Strategies evolved through more learning cycles, not rushed decisions	• Time between strategy drafts • Number of iterations before executive review • Earlier surfacing of risks and assumptions • Number of late-stage reversals or rework	Faster learning cycles led to stronger, more resilient strategies

Misty used AI as a thinking partner, and amplified her natural *traits* by pairing the right *tasks* with the right *tools*.

From Intuition to Decision

Combining human intuition with machine capability unlocks a new cognitive workflow:

**Organizing intuition → Generating structured strategy →
Making higher-quality decisions**

When AI stops being "a tool you use" and becomes "a partner you think with" leaders report significant acceleration in their outcomes:

- preparing research for a board presentation: **6 hours → 1.5 hours**
- writing department-wide updates: **3 hours → 30 minutes**
- high-stakes meeting summaries: **1 hour → 10 minutes**

These gains compound over time, but the bigger win is greater leadership clarity, confidence, and presence.

Four Everyday Thinking Strategies

In time-poor, high-stakes environments, executives need reliable thinking strategies they can apply under pressure. These four are designed to help you leverage AI as a thinking partner—not a productivity hack—and are used most consistently by high-performing leaders.

Each answers a different leadership question you face daily. This isn't about creating better prompts. It's about rehearsing judgment every day, so you're well prepared for critical moments. More advanced examples are available at artificialorganizations.com.

Strategy 1. Clarify: What am I actually deciding?

Purpose: Turn messy, fast-moving thoughts into a clear decision frame.

Deliverable: A one-page view of what matters, what's at risk, and what happens next.

Example Prompt (Goal–Output–Warnings–Context):

> **Goal**: Clarify the decision I'm facing.
>
> **Output**: A structured summary with key decisions, risks, and three options for next steps.
>
> **Warnings**: Don't invent facts or assumptions. Call them out explicitly if they appear.
>
> **Context**: These are my rough, unstructured thoughts about this **[initiative/issue]**, captured as [**voice note/transcript/ bullet points/notes/document**].

This strategy is how intuition becomes visible. You're asking AI to impose structure faster than you can.

Strategy 2. Challenge: What am I assuming or missing?

Purpose: Surface blind spots before they show up in the room.

Deliverable: A short list of assumptions, risks, and questions to test.

Example Prompt (Goal–Output–Warnings–Context):

> **Goal**: Pressure test my thinking before others do.
>
> **Output**: Key assumptions, blind spots, and risks I should address.
>
> **Warnings**: Be direct. Don't soften feedback or default to agreement. I'm preparing for an executive team discussion.
>
> **Context**: I'm thinking aloud about this **[initiative/issue]**, captured as **[voice note/transcript/bullets/notes/ document]**.

This strategy is your anti-groupthink mechanism. AI spots patterns and inconsistencies executives don't always see under pressure.

Strategy 3. Create Options: What paths are available?

Purpose: Move from debate and circling to real choice.

Deliverable: Three distinct paths forward, with trade-offs and decision triggers.

Example Prompt (Goal–Output–Warnings–Context):

> **Goal**: Generate clear strategic options.
>
> **Output**: Three options with pros, cons, and the trigger that would make each the right choice.
>
> **Warnings**: Avoid false precision. Focus on directional clarity, not perfect answers.
>
> **Context**: Here's the situation and constraints we're facing with this **[initiative/issue]**, captured as **[voice note/ transcript/bullets/notes/document]**.

This strategy helps leaders regain momentum. Instead of arguing in the abstract, you compare real options and decide with intent.

Strategy 4. Commit: What do I decide, by when?

Purpose: Translate thinking into action.

Deliverable: A clear decision, rationale, risks, and deadline.

Example Prompt (Goal–Output–Warnings–Context):

> **Goal**: Move from analysis to commitment.
>
> **Output**: The decision to make, why it matters, what happens if I delay, and the next step.
>
> **Warnings**: Force a decision. If more information is needed, define exactly what and by when.
>
> **Context**: Based on the analysis so far this **[initiative/issue]**, captured as **[voice note/transcript/bullets/notes/document]**.

This strategy delivers clarity, which translates into confidence.

The Trade-Offs:
What AI Is Great at—and What It's Not

Let's be frank. AI works as a thinking partner only when you understand the boundaries.

AI is great at:

- structure: turning scattered ideas into models, narratives, and plans
- pressure testing: surfacing assumptions, risks, and second-order effects
- perspective-switching: testing different stakeholder lenses
- momentum: moving from hunch to decision-ready options quickly

AI is not great at:

* truth: it can be confidently wrong—you still own judgment
* context: poor inputs lead to invented gaps
* politics and nuance: it can't feel the room or doesn't know the history

The goal isn't to outsource thinking. It's to upgrade it.

AI can expand your thinking, but it will sometimes produce confident inaccuracies. Your role is to interrogate, validate, and decide. You can delegate analysis. You cannot delegate accountability.

The Power Move: Train AI to Challenge You

As you go deeper with these tools, stop treating AI as something you *use* and start shaping it into something that thinks with you—and challenges you. This happens in two ways.

Explicit settings (tell it once)

Define your role, tone, structure, and decision style up front.

> Act as my executive thought partner.
>
> I'm a **[role]**.
>
> Structure outputs as **[bullets/memo/decision tree]**.
>
> Use a **[direct, candid]** tone.
>
> Default to surfacing trade-offs and risks.

Implicit settings (train it over time)

Every correction teaches the model how you think.

> Make this sharper.
>
> Push back harder.
>
> Too long. Give me the decision.

Over time, AI anticipates your judgment, not just your requests.

Case Study: Never Walk into a High-Stakes Room Unprepared CEO-Bot

One of my favorite examples comes from a senior leader working with a CEO known for rigorously challenging their team.

Every meeting felt high-stakes. Every decision carried weight. Meeting time windows were small, and expectations were high. The leader felt constant pressure to anticipate objections and gain buy-in for decisions, often over-preparing at the expense of other priorities.

So we built a simple helper, a CEO-bot that was trained on:

- the CEO's tone
- behavioral patterns
- challenge style
- common objections
- how they processed information
- how they pushed back on strategy
- what excellence looked like in meetings

This wasn't about gaming the CEO. It was about showing up prepared and more thoughtful, confident, and resilient.

Before major meetings, the leader fed raw drafts, bullets, or voice notes into the CEO-bot. The bot pushed back—hard. It surfaced inconsistencies, exposed weak logic, and revealed where conviction was missing. By the time of the meeting, the leader had already navigated multiple rounds of challenge.

That's what training AI to think like you—or like those who challenge you—unlocks: **a high-quality, safe space to prepare, reflect, and refine your perspective with productive criticism and without unintended consequences.** When leaders understand this, their performance spikes.

Leaders who rehearse judgment privately excel publicly.

The Power of a Partner for Structuring Thoughts

As a thinking partner, AI expands your cognitive range and performance. It lets you safely explore ideas, pressure test decisions before acting, sharpen instincts, and build conviction before stepping into high-stakes situations.

This is the quiet revolution happening within executive teams everywhere. Leaders are no longer thinking alone. They're testing, iterating, and improving their thinking against the toughest audience they can imagine—so they present only high-quality, high-conviction strategies worthy of limited time and attention. They show up as stand-out contributors and as colleagues you want to work with on hard problems.

The leaders who embrace this now will outperform, out-innovate, and outpace the rest. Will you be among them?

Exercise: CTSA — Capture, Transcribe, Synthesize, Act

Take one messy idea, something sitting in your head that you haven't had time to work through. It could be:

- a project you're avoiding
- a strategic shift you're considering
- a tough conversation
- a hunch you haven't validated
- an idea from the commute you never captured

Step 1: Capture the raw thinking.

Record a 30–60 second voice note. Don't edit. Don't structure. Just get it out.

Step 2: Transcribe and paste into AI.

Step 3: Use this prompt to synthesize your thinking.

> **Goal:** Turn raw thinking into decision clarity.
>
> **Output:** A structured view with:
>
> - decisions
> - risks
> - opportunities
> - next steps
> - assumptions and blind spots
> - three optional paths forward
>
> **Warnings:** Don't invent certainty. Label assumptions clearly. Challenge my thinking. Don't agree by default.
>
> **Context:** These are my raw, unfiltered thoughts. I'm thinking out loud, not deciding yet.

Step 4: Review the output.

Look for what surprises you, not what confirms you.

Step 5: Ask one follow-up question.

What am I not considering?

Step 6: Make your decision and act.

That's it. Five minutes. One breakthrough.

Before You Move Ahead, Reflect for One Minute

The last three chapters have helped you build decision velocity and decision advantage:

- Capture collapses context rebuild.
- Synthesis reduces decision latency.
- Rehearsal strengthens conviction.
- Action compounds advantage.

If you apply this system consistently, you'll exhibit three essential leadership behaviors:

1. You express greater clarity of thought.

2. You make calls more quickly.

3. You revisit fewer decisions.

The resulting leverage is what separates high-performing leaders from merely busy ones. Putting this system into deliberate, daily practice is how you widen the gap with your competitors and pull away.

— PART III —

INSTALL JUDGMENT INFRASTRUCTURE

> "Judgment doesn't scale through willpower. It scales through infrastructure."

Personal sharpness is fragile. It depends on energy, attention, and time. Infrastructure endures.

Here you design a Personal AI Stack aligned to your decision responsibilities. You convert recurring executive work into ExecutiveGPT workflows, and standardize decision shape across high-stakes contexts. Guardrails define what remains non-delegable human judgment, and aligned to compliance, confidentially and asset ownership for your workplace. Measurement shifts attention from activity to outcomes over output.

Decision velocity becomes structural. Decision advantage becomes repeatable.

CHAPTER 6

DESIGN YOUR PERSONAL AI STACK

*High-performing leaders don't think
in tools. They think in systems.*

In Chapter 4, you learned how AI sharpens research and decision-making—not by producing more information, but by improving synthesis, judgment, and clarity. In Chapter 5, you saw a deeper shift: AI as a thinking partner with which to explore half-formed ideas, pressure test instincts, and regain the thinking space most leaders have lost.

Here's the uncomfortable truth: If you stop there, none of it survives contact with your calendar. Clear thinking doesn't compound if it isn't captured. Better prompts don't matter if you can't construct or find them when pressure hits. Insight dies quickly without a system to move it forward. This is the point at which most leaders stall—not because AI doesn't work, but because they never design a system that's fully integrated into their day to day.

In this chapter, we'll create your **personal AI stack**: the tools, workflows, and habits that make this way of thinking portable, repeatable, and embedded in how you lead.

The Real Promise (and the Real Risk)

Leaders don't dream about AI tools. They dream about more space to think, more time on meaningful work, more energy for the problems only they can solve. They also dream about getting more of their personal time back.

AI can deliver that, but only if you stop treating it like a collection of features and start treating it like **infrastructure for how you work**.

Most leaders never fully make that shift. They experiment. They dabble. They get moments of value. And then it all fragments.

Where Leaders Go Wrong

From all my conversations, coaching, and collaborations with CEOs, C-suite leaders, and senior operators as they build their AI stacks, the failure pattern is consistent. Leaders go wrong when they:

- play with too many tools at once
- chase the latest release instead of outcomes
- focus on features instead of systems of work
- end up with a set of experiments, not a coherent stack

The market makes this worse. Tool vendors are loud, well-funded, and constantly battling for attention. Every platform claims to be "the one". Every update promises breakthrough productivity.

The moment you start exploring AI, you're exposed to an overwhelming landscape:

- personal assistants and writing tools
- productivity and work management tools
- meeting and memory AI
- content creation tools
- automation platforms
- research engines
- AI agents and builders

Each category makes sense on its own. Each has best-in-class options. Each solves a real problem. That's the trap.

Recommended AI Tools and Agents

High-leverage, low-barrier AI tools that are especially useful for strategy, productivity, communication, and decision-making.

Personal Assistants + Writing	ChatGPT	Claude AI	Google Gemini	Perplexity
Work System	Notion	Microsoft Copilot	Superhuman	Google Workspace
Meeting AI + Memory AI	Otter.AI	Fathom	Fireflies.ai	Granola
Content Creation	Canva	ChatGPT	Midjourney	Descript
Automation + Workflows	Zapier	Make	OpenAI Assistants	n8n
Insights + Research	Perplexity AI	Elicit	Glean	Scite.ai
AI Agents + Builders	OpenClaw	CrewAI	LangChain	AutoGen

For the most up-to-date recommended AI tools and agents, visit artificialorganizations.com.

Once you start mapping tools by category, it becomes dangerously easy to believe the answer is coverage: one or two tools per box. Leaders very quickly end up with sprawling tool matrices:

- overlapping assistants
- parallel research engines
- competing automation layers

Even on paper, it's unmanageable. Never mind integration, data consistency, or remembering which tool to use, when, and why. The result isn't leverage. It's cognitive overload and the spiraling cost of subscriptions.

Leaders spend more time:

- deciding which tool to use
- reentering the same information
- questioning outputs they don't fully trust
- abandoning tools that never quite stick

Eventually, many conclude that "AI is interesting, but not quite there yet."

The technology isn't the problem. The approach is. **AI adoption breaks down when leaders start with tools** instead of traits and tasks.

Start Where the Work Is

High-performance leaders don't think in tools. They think in systems that define:

- what outcomes matter
- what decisions the system should support
- how information is captured, transcribed, synthesized, and acted on
- how work flows from end to end
- how impact scales over time

The starting point is never the matrix. It's you: your natural traits, your highest-leverage tasks, and the moments when friction steals your time and attention. You need to think big—but start small.

Thinking big without starting small is how boards approve million-dollar AI initiatives in minutes, based on buzzwords instead of ROI. BCG's 2025[1] study found **74% of companies stuck in Proof of Concept (PoC) purgatory**—experimenting with AI, but making no measurable progress. Real change starts when leaders model new ways of working—first for themselves.

Case Study: Scaling Beyond Yourself Without Losing the Personal Focus Andrew Phillips, CTO of Skyscanner

Skyscanner operates at serious scale:

* 160+ million monthly users
* 1,200+ employees
* billions of price checks every day

As CTO, Andrew Phillips sits at the center of that complexity.

What's striking about Andrew isn't his technical depth. It's how personal his approach to AI has been. He didn't start with a mandate, roll out a framework, or declare a strategy. He started with a simple question: **Is this actually making my day better?**

Like most senior leaders, Andrew's days were dense with meetings: board discussions, leadership syncs, architectural reviews, external conversations. They were high stakes, high context, and high cognitive load. The struggle wasn't lack of information. It was **holding it all in his head**, switching contexts fast, and still showing up fully present and prepared.

Andrew began experimenting in the flow of real work. Some experiments worked. Many didn't. And that was the point.

---

1. Boston Consulting Group. AI at Work: Is the Era of Experimentation Over? Boston: Boston Consulting Group, 2025. https://www.bcg.com/publications/2025/ai-at-work -is-era-of-experimentation-over.

Trying, Failing, and Saying So Out Loud

Andrew didn't find the right tools quickly. What makes this story powerful is that he **shared openly with his leadership and technology teams**:

- what he was trying
- where he felt tools fell short
- when outputs felt generic
- when the overhead wasn't worth it

As Andrew put it, "I kept asking myself where this genuinely helped, where it distracted, and where humans absolutely needed to stay in the loop."

There was no pretense of mastery. That humility mattered. It gave teams permission to experiment without fear. AI stopped being a performance expectation and became a shared learning space.

By the time AI conversations broadened across Skyscanner, they weren't abstract. They were grounded in lived experience. That's how scaling actually works—not by pushing change down, but by pulling understanding up.

The Real Lesson

Andrew's story is a reminder of something many leaders forget: You don't scale impact by starting with scale. You scale impact by starting with yourself. You do it by being curious, trying new approaches in the flow of real work, being honest about what's not working, and sharing what you learn—even when it's imperfect.

That's how you improve performance *and* presence at the same time. And that's how personal experimentation becomes organizational capability—without ever losing the human center.

The Sequence That Works

Designing your AI stack isn't a one-time decision. It's an ongoing practice.

The sequence matters:

Think big → Start small → Learn fast → Iterate

You don't pick tools first. You start with traits and tasks.

Ask yourself:

- How do I naturally generate insight: talking, writing, sketching, debating?
- Where does my time actually go each week?
- Which tasks create disproportionate value when done well?

Only then do tools enter the picture.

Then after each effort, ask: Is this making my decisions structurally stronger?

Your response will determine whether you commit, pause, or pivot and try something else.

How I Built My Stack (One Tool at a Time)

My natural *trait* is talking: I do it to think, problem-solve, and make decisions with the leaders I work with. So the highest-leverage *task* for me was meetings. Whether coaching executives, working with founders, or supporting portfolio companies, meetings are where information, insight, and decisions are generated. They're also where enormous value is lost.

Given this trait and task, the tool was obvious: a meeting assistant to record, capture, and transcribe.

That single choice unlocked my first workflow:

**Pre-meeting prep → Capture → Transcribe →
Synthesize → Act→ Follow-up → Weekly recap**

Meetings became data assets. From there, stacking happened naturally:

- Transcripts enabled synthesis.
- Synthesis surfaced patterns.
- Pattern recognition informed better decisions.
- Better decisions delivered extraordinary results.

Work management followed, as did greater clarity in communication—concise strategy summaries, clear actions, and owners automatically assigned in work management systems.

From there the stack expanded naturally into content creation: transcripts became presentations, follow-ups turned into tasks, ideas became draft articles or board artifacts, weekly reviews rolled into dashboards, and even short video recaps for teams and investors.

That fueled performance, results, and further iteration. Automation came last—only once the workflow felt right.

I went from one tool to five, down to three, and up to fourteen. Then back down and up again. The stack may keep changing, but the logic doesn't:

Traits → Tasks → Tools

My Personal AI Stack

High-leverage, low-barrier AI tools that are especially useful for strategy, productivity, communication, and decision-making.

Personal Assistants + Writing	ChatGPT	Claude AI	
Productivity	Notion	Superhuman	
Meeting AI + Memory AI	Otter.AI		
Content Creation	Canva	Descript	Riverside
Automation + Workflows	n8n	Zapier	Make
Insights + Research	Perplexity AI		
AI Agents + Builders	Adept	Reka	

To see my latest AI Stack, visit artificialorganizations.com.

Sidebar: Breadth and Depth

Most executives operate within constraints. Your company may be all-in on Microsoft, Google, or some other platform. That's your **breadth** layer: broad ecosystems designed to provide a diverse portfolio of products and services, spanning several major areas of work, that function reasonably well. With Microsoft, for example, that includes Microsoft 365, Teams, Github, Co-pilot, Azure, and more. You pay one major licensing fee for the platform.

Alongside that lives **depth**: niche tools that do one job exceptionally well. Take meetings as an example. Enterprise platforms can record and summarize meetings, but a tool like Otter.ai or Granola excels at transcription quality, speaker recognition, and recall. It's built for that single job, and it outperforms breadth layer products every time. You pay per tool, meaning your stack is a collection of individual subscriptions.

- Neither approach is right or wrong. What matters is understanding the trade-off:

- Platforms provide coverage and compliance.

- Niche tools enhance performance and precision.

Your personal stack often blends both. You work within enterprise constraints while selectively layering niche tools that deliver the most leverage. The heuristic is simple: **use breadth for consistency and depth for excellence.**

The Compounding Effect of Stacking

What makes stacks powerful isn't any single tool. It's compounding. Executives I coach consistently report:

- 6–10 hours saved per week
- 40–60% increase in decision velocity
- 30–50% decrease in prep and follow-up time
- clearer thinking under pressure
- better stakeholder feedback
- fewer dropped balls

People show up differently when meetings result in progress instead of exhaustion. You can be fully present when you're not carrying unfinished admin in your head. This boosts not just personal productivity, but high performance for the company.

Wharton's 2025 Enterprise AI Adoption Report[2] showed the leading 6% of companies globally—defined by where AI initiatives are resulting in >5% EBITA returns—are achieving:

- 15–25% revenue acceleration
- 73% faster time-to-market
- 40% reduction in decision-making errors
- 2.3x valuation relative to industry peers

Company transformation starts with individual transformation. It all begins with how you work.

---

2. Puntoni, Stefano, Prasanna Tambe, and Jeremy Korst. Accountable Acceleration: Gen AI Fast-Tracks Into the Enterprise. Philadelphia: Wharton Human-AI Research and GBK Collective, October 2025.

Common Risks

There are real risks you need to monitor and measure when designing your AI stack, so it's very important to define the desired outcomes before you start using the tools.

Over-automation too early

Automating before a workflow is proven just scales uncertainty.

Start small—and manual. Use a meeting assistant, download the transcription, upload it to an LLM of choice, run a prompt from your Prompt Library, and evaluate the results. Once you see ongoing utility, automate with confidence.

Poor tool fit

Buying hype creates switching costs.

I've watched boards approve enterprise-wide AI licenses for 4,000 at $30 per person per month in minutes. Months later, usage is patchy, outcomes are vague, and the tool is too big to roll back. That's thinking big and starting big.

Data fragmentation

Building sprawling AI stacks without direction creates chaos.

When every team picks its own AI tools, information scatters and context disappears. Leaders spend more time reconstructing reality than deciding what to do next.

Set a clear default path. Then allow exceptions where performance truly improves.

The lure of novelty

Discipline beats novelty every time.

The leaders who get real leverage from AI don't chase every new capability. They are clear about outcomes, patient in design, and deliberate in how they build. That's how stacks compound instead of collapsing.

Exercise: Your First Stack Decision

Answer these five questions—honestly:

1. What is one high-leverage task that consumes time every week but doesn't require your full creativity?

2. Which natural trait do you rely on most to do great work: talking, writing, visualizing, synthesizing, etc.?

3. What single moment in your workflow would benefit most from capture or recall?

4. If you designed an end-state system for this task, what would "better" look like in 90 days?

5. What is the smallest experiment you could run this week: one trait, one task, one tool, one workflow?

Write down your responses. Start there.

The Stack Test

If you removed your AI stack tomorrow:

- Would your decisions slow down?
- Would your preparation quality drop?
- Would your clarity suffer?

If the answer to each of these questions is no, you don't have a stack. You have experiments.

Experiments entertain curiosity. Stacks boost performance.

CHAPTER 7

TURN YOUR ROUTINES INTO AI WORKFLOWS

Leverage doesn't come from executing tasks more productively. It comes from performing the work that matters—consistently better.

You have a stack. Now what?

A stack without routines is fragile. A routine without workflows doesn't scale. And a workflow without intention becomes automation theater.

The real leverage doesn't come from executing tasks more productively. It comes from developing better-quality work habits or rituals. It comes from redesigning how decisions move through your system and **consistent higher performance**. Most leaders have never mapped that flow.

In this chapter, we'll turn your **routines into AI workflows**, repeatable systems that scale your impact without scaling your workload.

Remember, transformation doesn't start with technology. It starts with **how *you* work**—and spreads to your teams and the larger organization. As a leader, this is how your one small step can have a systemic-level impact.

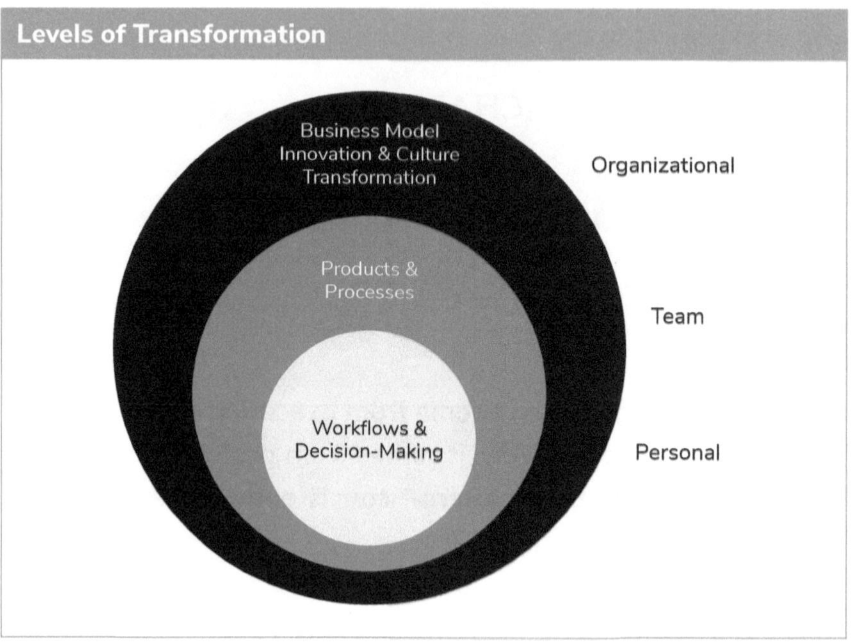

Personal Transformation: Workflows and Decision-Making

This covers personal productivity, higher performance, and better judgment. At this level, AI increases:

- **decision velocity**—how quickly you can move from signal to choice

- **decision advantage**—how well informed and pressure tested those choices are

Decisions are one part of the equation. The other is accelerating the **end-to-end workflows** that support your executive role.

Next, you will design your **first end-to-end workflow**: a small, automated system that supports how you show up, week after week.

Team Transformation: Products and Processes

When a personal workflow becomes repeatable, it becomes shareable. This is where an executive workflow turns into:

- a team habit
- a departmental assistant
- or a reusable process

This is how individual productivity scales to team capability—and sometimes results in new internal or external products.

Organizational Transformation: Business Model and Culture

At this level, workflows become pilots, pilots become systems, and systems reshape how the company operates—and occasionally what the company sells.

Although this book does not cover organizational transformation, you need to see the arc—because achieving personal transformation gives you a hands-on preview of what's possible across your organization.

If you don't start experimenting personally, you'll never change organizationally.

Why Workflows Matter (Not Tools)

AI mastery doesn't scale by adding more tools. It scales by **stacking behaviors.** Once you move beyond isolated tasks and start building end-to-end workflows, something shifts:

- You start recognizing your role as a system.
- You see where information breaks down.
- You notice where judgment—not data—is the bottleneck.
- You spot automation opportunities without forcing them.

This is the moment leaders move from *using AI* for personal transformation to *leading with AI* for organizational transformation.

This is **the next frontier of leadership leverage.**

Start Small. Start Personal. Role Model It.

I don't ask executives to "transform their organization." I expect them to transform **themselves**, to challenge how they've worked to date, to unlearn, relearn, and create breakthroughs in behavior and mindset.

I ask leaders to build **one working, end-to-end, AI-augmented workflow** that matters to their week. Something real and reusable that improves outcomes immediately—not a demo or prototype. A working executive function.

Doing this creates three immediate effects:

- Strengths and limitations surface quickly.

- The technology becomes tangible for both you and your team.

- Confidence replaces anxiety.

When leaders role model this—calmly, visibly, without hype—it gives everyone else permission to experiment.

The Executive Decision Engine

Almost every executive workflow follows the same underlying pattern:

Capture → Summarize → Classify → Distribute → Track

You already do this manually. AI collapses the friction—and often improves the quality.

1. Capture

Where raw thinking shows up:

- meeting notes (Zoom, Teams, Otter)

- voice memos

- Slack threads

- emails

- CRM notes

Perfection doesn't matter. Consistency does.

2. Summarize

This is where AI earns its keep:

- turning noise into signal
- surfacing what matters
- helping you research your own work

This isn't outsourcing thinking. It's organizing it.

3. Classify

High-performing leaders don't just generate insight—they structure it:

- themes
- actions
- owners
- risks
- decisions

This is execution discipline.

4. Distribute

Insight is useless if it stays in your head:

- Slack
- email
- CRM
- shared workspaces
- Chief of Staff/EA handoff

Clarity matters more than format. With this step, there's shared accountability.

5. Track

This is where workflows become systems that:

* auto-create tasks
* schedule calendar blocks
* log decisions
* make follow-ups visible

This is how intention becomes execution.

The First Workflow Every Executive Should Build: Weekly Business Review

Most executives already do a version of this manually—and hate how long it takes. It steals time from the executive function it's supposed to enable: decisions. This isn't from a lack of effort. What's missing is structure.

The Weekly Business Review isn't a meeting. It's a decision-making workflow that sits in the middle of your operating system. When it works well, it accomplishes three tasks at once:

* It aggregates reality from daily operations.
* It creates context for leadership decisions.
* It cascades cleanly into board-level reporting.

Over time, this workflow should be automatic. Here's how you prepare for Weekly Business Reviews.

Five minutes before the meeting

* Pull last week's review.
* Gather whatever inputs are available:
  - meeting summaries
  - Slack/email highlights
  - CRM snapshot
  - finance topline

- delivery KPIs
- risks, blockers, decisions needed

You don't need perfect data. You need enough **signal to support judgment.**

During the meeting

- Stay present.
- Focus on decisions, not note-taking.
- Trust your meeting assistant will record and capture.

This is where judgment happens.

Five minutes after the meeting

Add the context only you can provide:

- risks you're genuinely worried about
- edge cases the data doesn't show
- decisions that didn't land cleanly

Then run a reusable workflow that:

- synthesizes the week
- surfaces decisions and recommendations
- highlights risks and trade-offs
- publishes to a shared leadership space

What used to take an hour now takes minutes.

More importantly, the quality of these Weekly Business Reviews improves:

- People arrive prepared.
- Decisions are made faster.
- Patterns emerge over time.

One COO I worked with put it simply: "Our weekly review stopped being a status meeting and became a decision engine. Within a quarter, our board pack was basically done before we sat down to write it."

Most organizations run status meetings. Artificial organizations run decision engines. The difference compounds every week. That's decision velocity and decision advantage in practice.

Your First Custom GPT (ExecutiveGPT)

Once a workflow functions well, executives usually say, "I don't want to rebuild this every time." That's when you're ready for a Custom GPT. Not a chatbot or toy—a **reusable executive workflow**.

I call these **ExecutiveGPTs**. They're not about automation for its own sake. They're about setting yourself up for success—consistently.

An ExecutiveGPT is a **stable set of instructions** run against **fresh inputs**. The structure stays fixed (e.g. the decision shape), but the data changes. That distinction matters.

A good ExecutiveGPT:

- does one executive job

- does it the same way every time

- increases confidence under pressure

Examples:

- Weekly Business Review GPT

- Board Prep GPT

- 1:1 Meeting Prep GPT

- Monthly Finance Hygiene GPT

When you lock structure into a reusable workflow, you're no longer reacting. You're building repeatable executive judgment. This is how personal workflows become leadership multipliers—and how authority scales.

Step 1. Decide What It's Allowed to Know

Inputs = Knowledge Base

Before writing a prompt, answer one question: **What information should this workflow see every time?**

Most GPTs fail here—not because of prompting, but because of weak inputs or wrong access.

For a Weekly Business Review, inputs might include:

- meeting transcripts
- Slack/email highlights
- CRM snapshot
- finance topline
- delivery KPIs
- risks and decisions

Think of this as designing your **executive information diet**. Your GPT is only as good as the signal you feed it—week after week. Leverage the data assets you're creating each minute of your day!

Step 2. Lock the Structure

Once inputs are clear, lock the structure, so it's reusable.

Remember, use a simple Goal–Output–Warnings–Context framework:

> **Goal:** what this workflow exists to do and for whom
>
> **Output:** exact format you require
>
> **Warnings:** what to avoid; when to flag uncertainty
>
> **Context:** this week's inputs

The instructions remain the same. Only the context changes. That's a workflow—not a one-off prompt.

Example: Weekly Business Review ExecutiveGPT

Goal: Produce a one-page Weekly Business Review (WBR) for the executive team.

Output:

- 5-line executive summary
- KPI table (this week vs. last week vs. target)
- top risks and blockers (owner, mitigation)
- decisions needed (options and recommendation)
- notable wins and customer signals

Warnings:

- no fluff
- no jargon
- cite assumptions
- highlight missing data

Context:

- last week's WBR
- meeting summaries
- Slack/email highlights
- CRM and finance snapshot

You can run this every week, whether you're using OpenAI, Copilot, Anthropic, or other tools.

Step 3. Create Guardrails

The most important part of an ExecutiveGPT isn't what it answers. It's what it refuses to answer.

You want explicit behavior. If there's:

- missing data, then call it out
- ambiguity, then ask a follow-up
- judgment required, then surface options, not certainty

This is decision support—not decision automation.

Step 4: Measure the Boring Stuff First

Don't overthink ROI at the outset. Focus on what's easy to measure first. Track:

- time to produce the output
- time to decision
- consistency week to week
- quality of conversations

When those improve, everything else follows. Leaders realize they're doing some of the best work of their life because they're working on the *right* problems. Time is focused on creative problem-solving over routine administrative work. The team recognizes that the bar for expectations and improved performance has been raised—and respond.

Case Study: Excellence in Employee Experience
Cassandra Pratt, CHRO of Progyny

One of the strongest examples of workflow-driven AI I've seen didn't start in engineering, IT, or data science. It started in HR.

Progyny is a public, NASDAQ-listed company and a global leader in fertility and family-building benefits. Under the leadership of Chief HR Officer Cassandra Pratt, the company scaled rapidly from roughly 50 employees to more than 850.

As the organization grew, Cassandra was focused on a familiar but difficult challenge: how to deliver a consistently high-quality employee experience at scale, without burning out the HR team.

Her intent wasn't to "add AI to HR." It was to improve how work flowed.

The Problem

Like most fast-growing companies, Progyny's HR team was spending a disproportionate amount of time on:

- repetitive questions
- policy lookups
- onboarding basics
- context switching between low-stakes and high-stakes employee needs

This work was important, but it wasn't where HR created the most value.

Cassandra's goal was clear:

- Give employees fast, accurate answers when questions are straightforward.
- Free HR professionals to spend more time and care on situations where judgment, empathy, and trust matter most.
- Be explicit about what answers not to guess, and escalate to HR team members immediately.

That framing matters. This was an employee experience strategy supported safely, not a throw-away test.

The Approach

Cassandra set the direction and guardrails:

- what questions could be answered automatically
- what topics should *never* be handled by a system
- how escalation to humans should work
- how quality, privacy, and trust would be maintained

Then she encouraged experimentation.

An intern took ownership of building and operating the first version of an HR Bot focused initially on benefits and onboarding. That detail is important. This didn't require rare expertise. This was about building capability with **clear intent, good boundaries, and real usage**.

The Solution

The HR Bot provided:

- always-on answers for common employee questions (leave, benefits, policies, org basics, etc.)
- responses grounded in a clearly defined knowledge base (information sources defined, managed, and sandboxed by HR)
- explicit escalation to a human for sensitive or ambiguous topics

But the most valuable feature wasn't the answers. It was the **questions**.

By tracking what employees actually asked:

- the team could see where policies were unclear
- where documentation was outdated
- what employees genuinely cared about

The questions informed future changes or adaption of company policies. Instead of guessing, HR knew exactly what needed to be improved. They could focus their limited resources on the highest-leverage tasks, and improve employee service and experience.

This created a continuous feedback loop:

**Employee questions → Knowledge updates →
Better experience → Clearer signal**

The Impact

The outcomes were quick and clear:

- Standard HR queries shifted from ~24-hour response times to near-instant answers.

- Repetitive interruptions to HR dropped significantly.
- HR time shifted from low-level support toward high-stakes employee conversations.

Across Progyny's broader AI adoption efforts:

- **92% of leaders** reported increased clarity of company HR policies
- teams saw **25–40% gains in communication efficiency with HR**
- HR training development cycles improved by **95%** (from roughly 48 hours to 30 minutes)

These weren't abstract AI metrics. They were **experience and efficiency gains employees could feel**.

These gains were won not through AI efficiency but through leadership clarity. HR stopped being reactive support and became structured judgment at scale.

A new employee, Cynthia, captured it perfectly when she joined one of our coaching cohorts at Progyny:

> "Today is my third day. Yesterday I spent the whole day talking to the HR bot . . . and I learned so much about where everything is, how to find what I need, what to do, who to reach out to. I surprised myself."

When Cynthia later met with HR, her questions were:

- more specific
- more personal
- more sophisticated

HR time was spent on what it actually mattered: creating amazing employee onboarding experiences.

That's the levels of transformation diagram in action:

- **Personal**: clear decision-making and workflows with guardrails
- **Team**: continuous process improvement on an internal product based on real usage
- **Organization**: faster onboarding, better employee experience, stronger culture

This was all possible not because of AI alone—but because a senior leader (with a valuable assist from an intern) redesigned how work flowed.

Exercise: Build One Workflow You'll Reuse Every Week

Now it's your turn. Pick one routine that's slow, fragmented, or over-resourced. Design it using:

Capture → Summarize → Classify → Distribute → Track

Start with:

* Weekly Business Review (WBR)
* board prep
* client follow-up + CRM update

Then ask: **What should this workflow answer instantly—and what should it never answer?**

This question forces clarity, boundaries, and trust.

Once you build one workflow personally, you'll start seeing opportunities—for yourself, the team, and the organization—everywhere.

CHAPTER 8

MEASURE AND MANAGE YOUR AI OPERATING SYSTEM SAFELY

Stop mistaking activity and output for progress.
Measure what matters.

If you're honest, AI has probably made you busier. Your calendar is full. Your teams are experimenting. Your dashboards look impressive. Yet, when you ask yourself, "Is this actually making me better?", the answer is harder to prove than it should be.

Most leaders don't have a productivity problem. They have a **measurement problem.**

AI transformations don't usually fail because the technology doesn't work. They stall because leaders lose the ability to tell whether they're actually improving—personally and as a team. Motion replaces progress. Activity replaces outcomes. Delay replaces judgment.

Phil Gilbert, who led IBM's business transformation across more than 400,000 people and the author of *Irresistible Change*,[1] has seen this pattern repeatedly. He shared with me:

> "We've slipped back into the old 'butts-in-seats' metric.
> We tell people to go use the new AI tools and then count
> how many do. Almost nobody asks whether those tools are

---

1. Phil Gilbert, *Irresistible Change: Smart Ideas to Accelerate Business Transformation* (Hoboken, NJ: John Wiley & Sons, 2023).

helping teams generate better outcomes—or how they're changing the way decisions actually get made."[2]

That regression, from measuring outcomes back to counting activity, is one of the main reasons so many AI initiatives stall.

Your AI Operating System becomes valuable when it's **measured, managed, and corrected**.

Informed boards—certainly the ones I'm on—won't ask whether you're using AI. They'll ask whether your judgment infrastructure is competitive.

Executive Presence

Before we talk about metrics, we need to talk about **presence**.

Presence is the ability to be fully engaged and focused in the current moment—with yourself and with others. It's an awareness of how you're working and what is and isn't working (or quietly getting worse). It's the intention to make time to think.

Great leaders don't just execute plans—they also reflect. They notice drift. They sense weak signals. They create space to think before problems harden into decisions that are expensive to unwind. AI can amplify that capability or erode it.

Jeff Bezos famously protects his thinking time through a deliberate, low-stimulation routine often referred to as "puttering,"[3] which he credits with improving his decision-making and overall energy. He operates on two tracks. While one track focuses on efficiency and known destinations, the other is dedicated to wandering—a process fueled by hunch, gut, and curiosity to discover what efficiency misses. These moments surface your human intuition.

---

2. Barry O'Reilly, "Irresistible Change for Business Transformation with Phil Gilbert," Unlearn Podcast, November 2025, https://barryoreilly.com/explore/podcast/irresistible-change-for-business-transformation-with-phil-gilbert/.

3. Stillman, Jessica. "Jeff Bezos's Secret to a Clear, Focused Mind Is 'Puttering.' Psychology Says He's on to Something." Inc., January 10, 2025. https://www.inc.com/jessica-stillman/jeff-bezos-secret-to-a-clear-focused-mind-is-puttering-psychology-says-hes-on-to-something/91256882.

Top performing leaders protect their thinking time because they know leverage lives there. They use it to:

- connect with themselves
- contemplate scenarios
- reframe problems
- discover opportunities
- make tough decisions

That's the real return.

Used well, AI creates headroom: faster insight, clearer trade-offs, better preparation. Used poorly, it floods leaders with output and additional noise, dulling judgment.

Measurement and management aren't about control but about staying aware in a system that now moves faster than human instinct alone can manage.

From Time Spent to Signal Strength

Most productivity systems still reward effort:

- hours worked
- meetings attended
- emails sent
- documents produced

When drafting, summarizing, and analyzing approach zero marginal cost, **volume means nothing**. Output explodes, but value often doesn't.

Judgment systems break productivity models. What matters instead is signal:

- how quickly you notice meaningful change
- how clearly you frame the real decision
- how decisively you act with imperfect information
- how much time you protect for thinking that only you can do

In the age of intelligence, leadership performance is measured by **judgment under compressed time and pressure**.

The Decision Cycle

To measure properly, we need to be explicit about how leaders actually make decisions.

Every meaningful executive decision, whether strategic or operational, follows the same basic loop:

Sense → Think → Decide → Act

You sense what's changing. You think through options and trade-offs. You decide what to do. You act and observe what happens next.

Decision velocity and decision advantage are the twin engines of AI-augmented leadership. You measure both with this loop, which runs continuously.

When AI is helping, it **tightens this loop**: you sense earlier, think more clearly, decide sooner, and act with confidence. When AI is hurting, it **distorts the loop**: flooding you with data, clouding judgment, paralyzing decisions, and delaying action.

That's why the most important metrics are **decision metrics**.

Let's start with the **failure signals that tell you when AI is lying to you**.

Sense: Activity Inflation

Although the number of prompts, tools, and dashboards increase, warnings do not come earlier, patterns are no clearer, and surprises are no fewer.

If AI hasn't improved your ability to anticipate potential high-impact situations—earlier and with less effort—then sensing hasn't improved. More data with the same surprises is not progress. It's noise.

Think: Output Without Outcome

Documents are generated, summaries are produced, and options are presented, but the real question remains fuzzy. Trade-offs aren't clearer, and decisions don't feel easier. Analysis got faster but not better.

Decide: Latency Masking

Preparation improves and slides look sharper, but decisions aren't made. If meetings still end with, "Let's come back to this," AI hasn't improved decision-making. It has simply raised the standard of delay.

Act: Experiment Saturation

Pilots are everywhere but do not scale. Low kill-rates aren't a sign of success. They indicate that no one is learning fast enough to make hard, decisive calls. Action without consequence breaks the loop—and burns budgets.

Across the Loop: Confidence Decay

Listen to leadership language. When sentences start with, "The AI says . . ." instead of "Here's the call . . .", judgment is being outsourced. AI should boost leadership confidence—not replace it. It should strengthen conviction during uncertainty. If it weakens ownership, your system is eroding authority.

When AI Looks Busy but Isn't Working

Most AI initiatives fail quietly—under a mountain of activity. Prompts multiply. Dashboards fill up. Pilots spread across the organization. From the outside, it looks like momentum, but nothing of value has changed.

This is the most dangerous phase of AI adoption: **high activity, low impact, and growing confidence that "we're doing AI."**

According to McKinsey's *State of AI 2025*[4], nearly **80% of organizations say efficiency is the primary objective of their AI initiatives.** Yet the companies generating the most value are the ones that **explicitly set growth and innovation outcomes alongside efficiency.** Those organizations are not only three times more likely to pursue transformative change, they are also more likely to report meaningful enterprise benefits—from revenue growth and competitive differentiation to

4. McKinsey & Company, The State of AI in 2025 (New York: McKinsey & Company, 2025), https://www.mckinsey.com/capabilities/quantumblack/our-insights/the-state-of-ai-2025.

improved customer satisfaction—than firms focused on cost reduction alone.

In short, leading organizations measure outcomes, not just activity. Volume feels like progress and output feels like momentum, but neither proves transformation. This isn't a tooling problem. It's a leadership measurement failure.

AI theater is the new corporate theater. Persisting in this act means falling even further behind competitors who are measuring outcomes and accelerating ahead.

Coaching Case Study:
Busy, Sophisticated, and Stuck

A senior executive I coached, who was part of a global leadership team, proudly described their AI rollout as having dozens of pilots, high adoption, and strong internal buzz. Yet when we reviewed the last quarter together, something was missing: no major decision had been made faster, no strategic call had changed, no risk had surfaced earlier. Everything looked modern, but nothing felt different.

We mapped their leadership work against the decision cycle.

- Sense: dashboards everywhere, but still surprised by escalations
- Think: AI summaries improved pre-reads, but trade-offs stayed implicit
- Decide: decisions deferred "until we have more data"
- Act: pilots accumulated, but few were deliberately stopped

The issue wasn't AI capability. It was **measurement blindness**. We introduced two simple metrics to start:

- time-to-decision for leadership meetings
- percentage of pilot experiments deliberately killed within 30 days

Within six weeks, behavior shifted. There were fewer pilots, but each had quantifiable progress. There were clearer calls made with more confidence.

Nothing magical changed. They simply stopped mistaking activity for progress and confusing scale for sophistication.

Measure What Matters: Personal and Team Outcomes

AI adoption is easy to measure; AI advantage is not. Most organizations track usage, licenses, and output volume. If you want to know whether AI is optimizing your leadership—or merely decorating your workflow—you must measure two levels:

- how you decide
- how your system moves

1. Personal Metrics: The Strength of Your Judgment

These metrics tell you whether AI is strengthening your decision-making or just accelerating activity.

Decision Velocity

- How long does it take you to move from signal to decision? From when an issue surfaces to its resolution? Days, weeks, or months?
- How much time do your meetings take? Are they shorter or longer?
- How many decisions do you make in meetings versus those you defer?

Decision velocity is about shortening the length of time between the question and the call. If your meetings end earlier, but your decisions are deferred, then velocity hasn't improved.

Decision Advantage

- How robust are your decisions under pressure?
- Are the trade-offs explicit?
- Are you surfacing and challenging assumptions?
- Are decision reversals decreasing?

If you frequently unwind decisions, then your synthesis is weak, no matter how fast you moved. Strong decision advantage means fewer rework loops and fewer "we need to revisit this" moments.

Time-to-Insight

- How quickly does raw data become usable intelligence that brings you clarity?
- Do you detect patterns earlier?
- Are you acting on leading indicators instead of lagging reports?
- After you act, how long before you know whether it worked?

Insight delayed is opportunity lost.

Decision Reversal Rate

- How often do you revisit or unwind major calls?

Reversals are expensive, both politically and financially. High reversal rates signal incomplete framing, weak challenge, or rushed consensus. AI should reduce backtracking, not increase it.

Publish Cadence

- How consistently do you externalize decisions, direction, and reasoning?

Clarity compounds when thinking is visible; if your team must guess your intent, you are moving too slow. Leadership isn't what you decide privately—it's what your team can act on independently.

Creative-to-Routine Ratio

- What percentage of your time is spent on judgment versus coordination? On creative problem-solving versus routine administrative tasks?
- Is AI creating space for you to frame problems, weigh trade-offs, and make hard calls? Or is it generating more output for you to review?

If your ratio hasn't shifted toward creative judgment, your system is misaligned.

2. Team Metrics: The Strength of Your System

Personal acceleration is meaningless if it doesn't scale. These metrics indicate whether your redesigned judgment is compounding across your teams and the organization.

Time-to-Decision

* Are issues resolved faster where they're happening? Or are decisions still escalating unnecessarily?

If decision velocity doesn't improve beyond you, you've built leverage for yourself but not for your teams or the organization

Decision Reversal Rate

* Are teams revisiting the same calls repeatedly? Or are decisions sticking?

High reversal rates indicate weak framing, unclear ownership, or insufficient challenge.

Experiment Kill Rate

* How quickly do weak ideas get shut down?

Healthy systems don't just generate experiments, they are decisive and terminate unviable ones early. Faster kill rates signal stronger synthesis and clearer thresholds.

Clarity of Priorities

* Can teams articulate the top three priorities without interpretation?

If AI is working, strategic clarity should increase. If confusion persists, the system hasn't improved—it's just louder.

Employee Confidence in Direction

* Do teams express greater conviction in decisions? Or more hesitation because "the AI suggested it"?

AI should strengthen ownership, not dilute it. If it weakens ownership, your system is eroding authority.

If your personal metrics improve but your team metrics do not, you are becoming faster, not better.

Artificial organizations emerge when judgment infrastructure scales.

AI increases output by default. It only optimizes leadership if decision quality improves and outcomes get better.

The AI OS Diagnostic

The table below is a **diagnostic tool**, not a scorecard.

It's designed to:

- reveal weak points in the decision cycle

- spark conversations

- identify where to intervene

It's not meant to be or provide:

- performance rankings

- precision instruments

- reasons to punish teams

Use this table to ask better questions.

The AI OS Diagnostic

Decision Cycle Stage	Healthy Signal	Warning Signal
Sense	Earlier pattern detection	More data; same surprises
Think	Clearer options and trade-offs	Faster analysis; same ambiguity
Decide	Fewer deferrals	Better decks; delayed calls
Act	Experiments scale or stop	Pilots pile up
Judgment	Leader owns the call	Deference to the model

If AI doesn't change behavior, it's decoration.

> ## Board-Level Sidebar: Questions Directors Should Ask About AI
>
> Use these questions to cut through AI theater in the boardroom:
>
> 1. Which decisions are materially different because of AI?
> 2. Where has time-to-decision actually shortened?
> 3. What AI experiments did we deliberately stop, and why?
> 4. How often does AI surface signals before issues escalate?
> 5. Where are leaders deferring judgment to models?
> 6. How much of the AI stack is reused versus reinvented?
> 7. What business outcomes improved, not just outputs?
> 8. Where did AI increase noise instead of clarity?
> 9. Which decision-making cycle stage is weakest across the organization?
> 10. If we removed AI tomorrow, what capability would we truly miss?
>
> If these questions feel uncomfortable, they're doing their job.

Lead Safely Without Slowing Down

Every powerful system needs constraints. This isn't about compliance. It's about **decision hygiene**.

Leaders should be explicit about:

- what information never enters the AI loop
- where human judgment is non-delegable
- what data exposure would damage trust if mishandled

Silence creates ambiguity. Ambiguity creates risk.

Treat security and privacy as leadership responsibilities, not IT concerns.

Keep the System and Data Fresh

Your AI Operating System is not set-and-forget. Models change. Context shifts. Your role evolves.

High-performing leaders regularly review their AI OS on a weekly or monthly cadence, asking:

- What decisions did AI accelerate?
- Where did it slow me down?
- What surprised me?
- What needs correction?
- How often am I refreshing my data sets?

Fresh systems and data stay useful. Stale systems eventually fail or, worse, lead you and your team to make decisions based on obsolete data.

Exercise: Establish Your Measurement Baseline

The leaders who win aren't those who adopt the most AI. They're the ones who measure judgment improvement relentlessly.

Before you optimize, observe.

1. **Reality Check**
   Which part of your decision cycle is weakest today: Sense, Think, Decide, or Act?

2. **One High-Leverage Task**
   Choose one weekly task where judgment matters more than speed. Map:

   - inputs
   - desired output
   - success signal

3. **One Metric**
   Fill in the blanks: If my AI OS is working, I should see ________________
   more often and ________________ less often within 30 days.
   That's enough to start.

You've Built Your Operating System

Step back and look at what you've constructed:

- Infrastructure: Your AI Stack provides you with thinking support and stability.

- Systems: Your workflows turn judgment into repeatable action.

- Control: Your measurement ensures speed doesn't erode quality.

Most leaders operate with tools. You operate with architecture. This is no longer experimentation. It's an executive operating system, one designed to increase decision velocity, strengthen decision advantage, and compound clarity over time.

From now on, you're leading in this age of intelligence.

PART IV

SCALE DECISION ADVANTAGE

"Judgment becomes advantage the moment it stops living in one leader and starts shaping how the organization decides."

Judgment that lives in one leader is fragile. Judgment that scales becomes advantage.

What matters now is not how clearly you think, but how clearly your organization decides. Time-to-decision shortens. Reversal rates decline. Weak initiatives are killed earlier. Ownership strengthens instead of deferring to the model.

This is where Judgment Infrastructure compounds—not as productivity gains, but as institutional performance. Decision velocity improves without sacrificing rigor. Decision advantage becomes visible in results, not activity.

Artificial organizations do not emerge from tools. They emerge when better judgment becomes the system. When you combine the best of human and machine intelligence for better outcomes.

CHAPTER 9

LEAD THE FUTURE: YOUR 5–15–30 ROADMAP

The strongest leaders aren't the ones with the answers. They're the ones willing to ask better questions and act on what they learn.

If there's one myth worth killing early, it's this: that leading in the age of AI requires knowing what's coming next.

It doesn't. No one knows how this plays out—not the vendors, the analysts, or the CEOs who sound most confident on stage. If you're waiting for perfect clarity before you act, you're already falling behind.

What matters now is whether your judgment infrastructure is competitive. Can you move from signal to decision at speed without losing rigor? Do you revisit fewer calls because your thinking was pressure tested up front?

What distinguishes effective leaders in the age of AI isn't foresight. It's having the combination of human lessons and machine capabilities compound. But first, you must participate. The only way to understand this technology is to use it. The only way to lead with credibility is to learn visibly. And the only way to scale responsibly is to start personally.

This chapter gives you a roadmap to build that advantage deliberately—without theater, without pretending, and without outsourcing what you're ultimately being paid for: judgment.

The goal isn't to "be good at AI." It's to build better judgment, faster learning loops, and stronger leadership presence as complexity increases. That's what differentiates AI-augmented leadership from legacy leadership that relies on past successes, expecting it to provide ongoing results.

No One Knows It All (and That's the Point)

The leaders who struggle most are often the most experienced. They've been rewarded for intuition, decisiveness, and pattern recognition. AI doesn't replace judgment; it exposes how judgment is formed. It surfaces assumptions, highlights gaps, and shows where instinct is strong and where it's guessing. That discomfort isn't a failure mode. It's the work. It is why people with solid information sourcing skills can outlearn and outperform leaders with long tenures in companies. It is why being an active participant and role modeling matters more than ever.

When leaders experiment openly—sharing what worked, what failed, and what they'd never do again—they give their organizations permission to learn without fear. Posturing drops, psychological safety rises, and progress accelerates. That's what great leadership looks like in this moment—and it has to start with you.

From Experience to Expertise

Experience used to compound automatically. Time in role meant better decisions, higher productivity, and stronger performance.

Today, experience only compounds when it's paired with feedback. AI provides that feedback—fast, objective, and often uncomfortable. If you're willing to engage with it honestly, it reveals patterns you missed, questions you didn't ask, and assumptions you didn't realize you were making. Leaders who lean into this don't lose authority. They gain range.

In coaching, I regularly see executives use AI as:

- a thinking partner to pressure test decisions before high-stakes meetings
- a mirror that surfaces conversational patterns across weeks of interactions
- a synthesizer that turns scattered signals into coherent insight

The shift is subtle but profound. You stop relying on memory and instinct alone, and start pairing them with evidence and perspective. That's the move from experience to expertise, from knowing it all to learning it all—fast. You're building judgment, speed, and results by combing human and machine intelligence.

Case Study: Learning Together When No One Has the Answers Stephen Franchetti, CIO of Slack

When the world shifted almost overnight in 2020, executive leadership was forced into unfamiliar territory: remote work at scale, new technologies, early signals that AI would fundamentally change how work gets done.

Stephen Franchetti, CIO of Slack, saw the challenge clearly, and reached out to me to see what we could do together to help leaders across North America[1]. This wasn't a problem any single leader or any single company could solve alone.

Executives everywhere were asking the same questions:

- How do we lead teams we no longer see every day?
- Which technologies actually matter and which are just noise?
- How do we experiment with AI responsibly while still running the business?
- What tools are accelerating work or creating more friction?
- How do we scale new ways of working without breaking trust, culture, or momentum?

There were no best practices, no proven playbooks, no experts with complete answers, so instead of manufacturing certainty, we chose a different path: we built a **community of learning.**

---

1. O'Reilly, Barry. "Slack: A More Connected and Resilient Technology Leadership Community. https://barryoreilly.com/explore/stories/slack/.

How We Approached the Problem

Working closely with Stephen and the team at Slack, we designed an environment where leaders could **learn their way forward together** in real time, under real constraints.

Slack became the connective tissue. Inside the community:

- Leaders from large enterprises and fast-growing companies showed up weekly.
- Topics were surfaced and upvoted by participants, not dictated from the top.
- Weekly sessions focused on current, lived challenges, not theory.
- Monthly Ask-Me-Anything (AMA) sessions were shaped entirely by the questions people were actually wrestling with.

The tone was intentional: no experts, no theater, no pretense. Leaders shared openly:

- what they were trying
- what worked
- what failed
- what surprised them
- what they would never do again

As patterns emerged, we formed **smaller working groups** around the toughest issues executives were facing, from decision-making in distributed teams to early AI experimentation, governance, and trust.

We also circulated **experience reports**: short, practical stories capturing how organizations were adapting in the moment, so others could learn without repeating the same mistakes.

The result wasn't alignment around a single answer. It was momentum and camaraderie.

What Changed

Over nine months, more than **200 Fortune 1000 technology leaders** engaged in a global learning community that included:

- a six-part leadership webinar series hosted by Slack
- 60+ CIOs and CTOs participating in focused working groups
- monthly AMAs driven by the community's real questions

Something subtle but powerful happened. Executives stopped asking: "What tool should we use?" and started asking: "What decisions are we trying to improve?" That shift changed everything.

The win wasn't simply community. It was shared decision patterns: leaders stopped talking about tools and **started trading decision-making systems**. That's how judgment scales across companies, not just within them.

Why It Worked

The success of the Slack community didn't come from better answers. It came from **embracing uncertainty together**.

No one had all the answers to the challenges created by the pandemic, remote work, or the acceleration of AI that followed. By taking small, visible steps within our own organizations, and then sharing those experiences openly, leaders moved faster *together* than they ever could alone.

As Stephen Franchetti put it:

> "Creating a global community of business and technology leaders has been one of the most rewarding things we've done—especially at a time when the world, and the way we worked, was changing so fast."

Slack didn't scale new ways of working, technology adoption, or AI experimentation through mandate. They scaled them through **shared learning**.

Why This Matters Now

This is the pattern that I continue to see work, especially with AI. Not expert-driven transformation or top-down rollouts, but leaders learning in public *together*. That's why I keep investing in communities where executives can explore, experiment, and share honestly in a safe, positive manner. The future isn't built by people who claim certainty. It's built by those of us who are willing to learn (and unlearn) out loud.

Beyond a case study, consider this your invitation to join our community at artificialorganizations.com.

The 5–15–30 AI Leadership Roadmap

Most leaders don't fail at AI because of intent. They fail because they don't sequence the work. They start with tools instead of identifying their natural traits and highest leveraged tasks. They run too many pilots without success metrics. They scale before role modeling.

The 5–15–30 roadmap exists to prevent that. It's not about transformation theater. It's about compounding behavior through disciplined learning, visible action, and clear signals of progress.

The roadmap unfolds in three phases:

- First 5 days: Build your personal OS for decision-making.
- Next 15 days: Expand and share your workflows.
- Final 30 days: Pilot, measure, and manage your OS.

Each phase builds credibility, capability, and confidence—in that order.

First 5 Days: Build Your Personal OS

Objective: Build credibility through action.

In the first five days, your job isn't to lead others. It's to change how *you* work.

Focus on three actions:

1. **Design your personal AI Operating System:** Develop one simple workflow that saves you time every week, whether it's meeting preparation, decision synthesis, or follow-up.

2. **Create a Weekly Business Review (WBR) GPT:** Use AI to summarize signals across your week: decisions made, risks emerging, and themes repeating.

3. **Publish personal productivity metrics:** Pick two or three metrics that define "better" for you and share them with someone you trust.

By Day 5, you should be able to show:

- **Prep and follow-up time decreased by 25–40%:** Measure one recurring forum (board meeting, ELT, investment review, weekly executive sync). If prep and follow-up time hasn't dropped by at least 25%, redesign the workflow.

- **Time-to-decision shortened in one recurring forum:** Pick one decision forum. Track the number of meetings or days required to finalize a decision. If you're not seeing at least a 20–30% reduction in decision cycle time, your synthesis is weak.

- **Fewer decision reopens:** Count how often decisions are revisited. If you're reopening the same decision twice within 30 days, your pressure testing isn't strong enough.

- **Weekly synthesis produced in <30 minutes:** Your WBR (or equivalent executive roll-up) should take under 30 minutes to generate and refine. If it still takes 60–90 minutes, your capture layer is broken.

- **External feedback from one peer or direct deport:** Ask directly, "Have you noticed a change in how I prepare, decide, or follow up?" If the answer is unclear or neutral, the shift isn't visible yet.

Day 15: Expand and Share

Objective: Move from personal wins to collective learning.
Widen the lens:

- Redesign one workflow end-to-end.

- Run a show-and-tell: what worked, what didn't, what surprised you.

- Start a small community of learning that is honest, regular, and practical.

This is where most leaders and, in turn, most organizations stall. The goal isn't perfection. It's visibility, transparency, and safety.

By Day 15, you should be able to demonstrate:

- **One workflow fully redesigned end-to-end**: Take one workflow (weekly executive review, investment memo prep, pipeline review, hiring calibration) and ask: Was cycle time reduced by 30–50%? Were there fewer "context rebuild" segments in meetings? Was a clear decision owner documented? If time shrinks but clarity doesn't improve, then you optimized speed but not judgment.

- **Team-level decision velocity improved:** Measure one team decision flow from the time an issue surfaced to when a decision was made. Did you achieve the targeted 20–40% reduction in this duration? If decisions still escalate unnecessarily, your architecture isn't scaling.

- **Reversal rate declined:** Track how often team decisions are revisited or rewritten. If the reversal rate hasn't dropped within 15–20 days, then framing is still weak.

- **One public show-and-tell delivered:** Document before and after the workflow. Are metrics shared openly? Have at least 3 peers adopted elements from the presentation? If the workflow is still private, it won't scale.

Final Day 30: Pilot, Measure, and Manage

Objective: Turn experiments into systems.

By Day 30, AI should feel less like a novelty and more like early-stage infrastructure. You should be able to prove:

- **Department-level decision cycle time reduced by 30–50%:** Have hiring approval cycles shortened? Are sales forecast decisions being made more quickly? Are budget reallocations processed in fewer review loops? If cycle time hasn't materially shifted, it's tool dabbling not transformation.

- **Experiment kill rate improved:** Has the time from experiment launch to kill decision shortened? Are faulty ideas being shut down faster? If you're still debating poor initiatives for weeks, synthesis is weak.

- **Clear governance boundaries published:** Have you documented and shared what AI is used for, what it's not used for, the escalation rules, and the human override expectations? If governance is vague, authority erodes.

- **Measurable gains in one of the twin engines:** Is there improvement in decision velocity (cycle time decrease of 30–50%) and/or decision advantage (reversals down, trade-offs clearer)? If neither has improved, the pilot has failed.

The Executive Scorecard

At the end of 45 days, you should be able to answer Yes to at least four of these:

- Is my prep time down by at least 30%?
- Do my recurring decision forums close issues more quickly?
- Have we revisited fewer decisions?
- Does my weekly synthesis take under 30 minutes?
- Is one team-level workflow 30–50% faster?
- Have we killed at least one weak initiative earlier than we would have before?
- Do my board or executive peers notice sharper trade-offs?

If you can't check four boxes, you don't have an operating system yet. You still have experiments.

Pilot Design Canvas: Executive-Level Workflows

Use Case & Tasks	Stakeholders	Tools
Decision Prep & Pressure Testing Prepare for high-stakes decisions (board, exec, M&A, major investments). Tasks include synthesizing inputs, surfacing assumptions, stress testing options, and anticipating objections.	Executive board members Executive peers	ChatGPT/ Claude Internal strategy docs Meeting transcripts
Personal Weekly Executive Reviews (WBR) Create a weekly roll-up of meetings, signals, risks, and themes. Tasks include summarizing conversations, spotting patterns, and identifying decisions and follow-ups.	Executive direct reports	Otter/Copilot/ Zoom transcripts ChatGPT/ Claude Email/ calendar data

Success Metrics	30-Day Signals to Accelerate	30-Day Signals to Kill or Redesign	Risks to Monitor
Decision cycle time decreases Fewer revisits of the same decision Clear articulation of trade-offs	Prep time reduced by 30–50% Meetings focus on decisions, not context Fewer "we need more info" follow-ups	Prep time has not reduced by at least 20%. Meetings still spend >50% of time rebuilding context. The same decision is reopened more than once. We stop and redesign the workflow.	Over-reliance on AI framing Confirmation bias if prompts aren't adversarial Using AI outputs without judgment
Time spent on weekly review decreases Improved clarity on priorities Faster follow-through on actions	Consistent weekly review produced in <30 min Clear top 3 priorities each week Fewer dropped actions	Weekly synthesis consistently takes >45 minutes. The top 3 priorities shift midweek without a new signal. Follow-through on actions has not measurably improved. We stop and redesign the capture, transcribe, and synthesize process.	Incomplete data if meetings aren't captured Noise outweighing signal Treating summaries as "truth" instead of inputs

(continued)

Pilot Design Canvas: Executive-Level Workflows (continued)

Use Case & Tasks	Stakeholders	Tools
Executive Communication & Narrative Shaping Draft and refine executive-level communications (board updates, org messages, strategy narratives). Work on clarity, tone alignment, and message consistency.	Executive board Leadership team Wider organization	ChatGPT/ Claude Past communications Company values/ strategy docs
Executive One-on-One Preparation & Follow-Through Prepare for recurring one-on-ones with direct reports and peers. Tasks include reviewing prior commitments, surfacing themes across past conversations, clarifying coaching intent, and capturing follow-ups.	Executive direct reports Executive peers	Otter/Copilot ChatGPT/ Claude Calendar and notes

Success Metrics	30-Day Signals to Accelerate	30-Day Signals to Kill or Redesign	Risks to Monitor
Draft iterations decrease Alignment across audiences improves Reduced misunderstanding or rework	Drafts completed in one sitting Fewer clarifying questions post-send Leaders reuse core narrative language	Draft cycles are not reduced by at least 30%. Stakeholders still request significant clarification post-send. Messaging feels more polished but less authentic. *We stop and redesign the framing and guardrails.*	Loss of authentic voice Over-polished but empty messaging Sensitive info leakage if guardrails aren't clear
Time spent preparing per 1:1 decreases Quality of coaching conversations improves Follow-through on commitments increase	Prep time reduced to <10 minutes Conversations focus more quickly on substance Fewer repeated issues across weeks	Prep time is not reduced by at least 30%. The same issues recur without resolution. Trust signals decline (hesitation around transcription, guarded responses). *We stop and redesign the norms and workflow.*	Over-instrumenting sensitive conversations Trust erosion if transcription norms aren't explicit Treating summaries as performance records instead of coaching aids

Artifacts That Make This Stick

Two scaffolds anchor this work:

1. Weeks Ahead: What am I preparing for?
2. Path Ahead: What decisions does this unlock?

Keep learning oriented toward forward motion, not retrospection. Pair them with a Pilot Design Canvas:

- use case and tasks
- stakeholders
- tools
- success metrics
- 30-day signals to accelerate
- 30-day signals to kill or redesign
- risks to monitor

This instills discipline without drag.

Where Leaders Go Wrong

After early momentum, I see the same failure modes:

- starting with tools instead of traits
- no metrics to define "better"
- too many pilots; no signals for success, kill, or redesign
- using AI for efficiency only
- scaling before role modeling

The fix isn't more strategy. It's better sequencing and shared learning.

Exercise: Design Your First 30 Days

Try your hand at your own 5–15–30 Roadmap:

1. Identify one executive workflow you own end-to-end.

2. Define what "better" looks like in two metrics.

3. Design a 30-day plan using the Pilot Canvas.

4. Decide who will see your work—and learn alongside you.

Leadership in the age of AI isn't about knowing the future. It's about building the capability to learn faster than it unfolds.

THE CHOICE YOU FACE

Let's return to the core idea of this book: Better outcomes don't come from humans alone. They don't come from machines alone. They come from **human judgment deliberately paired with machine intelligence**.

That combination is what improves decision quality, increases speed without sacrificing rigor, and produces better results under real operating conditions. Actual outcomes.

This book isn't about tool adoption or efficiency for its own sake. And it isn't about replacing leadership and judgment with automation.

The real promise of AI is leverage: clearer thinking, faster cycles of sense-and-decide, and stronger execution as complexity increases.

In the preface, I described the most valuable leader: not the one with the most data, but the one with the best judgment when the stakes are high and the information is incomplete.

AI doesn't replace leadership. It **amplifies it or exposes its absence**.

From Productivity to Performance and Presence

In the preface, I introduced a personal leadership progression:

Productivity → Performance → Presence

Most leaders approach AI at the productivity layer. They want:

- faster preparation
- quicker summaries
- fewer administrative tasks

And yes, that happens, but productivity is only the entry point.

When AI is applied deliberately, productivity transforms into performance.

- Decision cycles shorten.
- Trade-offs surface earlier.
- Reversals decline.
- Experiments end faster or scale beyond pilots.

You don't just move faster. You move outcomes. That's performance. But the highest level isn't productivity or performance. It's presence.

Presence is what happens when cognitive load drops: You walk into rooms prepared, not overloaded. You decide with conviction, not hesitation. Your authority comes from clarity, not control.

AI does not create presence. It creates the conditions for it. AI-augmented leadership enables and compounds presence.

Two Paths, One Decision

Earlier, we looked at the diverging paths of leaders who experiment with AI versus those who continue optimizing past systems. That curve wasn't illustrative—it was predictive.

One path compounds judgment: decisions get better, cycle times shorten, and results improve because leaders see trade-offs sooner and act with greater confidence.

The other path flattens—not because people stop working hard, but because the existing system can no longer keep pace with the environment it's meant to serve.

The gap between the two widens slowly at first, and then suddenly. This pattern is consistent among the executives I coach. The difference isn't intelligence, experience, or intent. The leaders who surge ahead aren't waiting for certainty. They're using AI themselves, learning in public, and honing judgment through use—not theory.

Over time, that learning compounds. And the opportunity cost of *not* doing it becomes a price too high to pay.

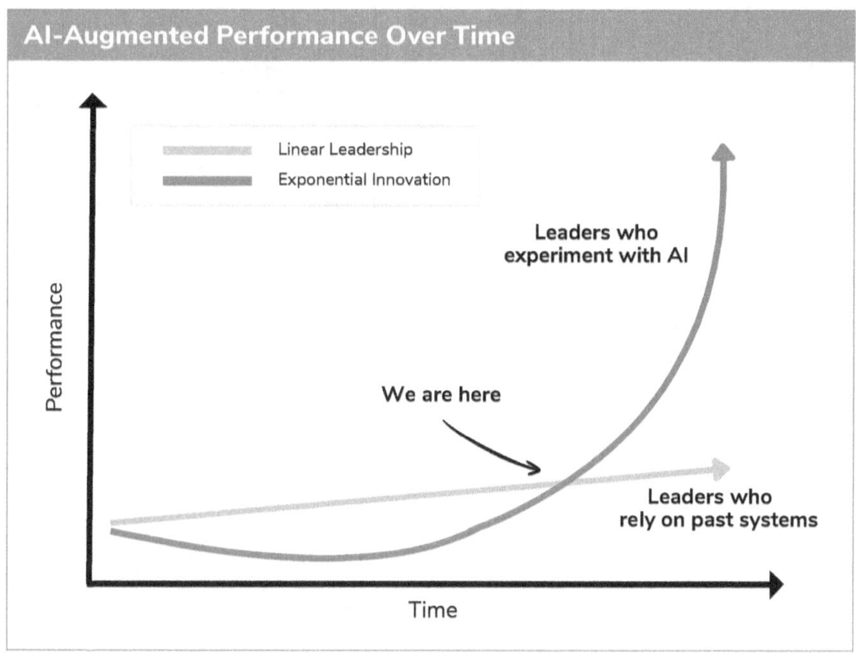

Time Back Was Not the Point. Leverage Is.

The most persistent misconceptions about AI is that its value lies in time saved, cost efficiency, and automation. It doesn't. Its value lies in how it changes what you do with your time.

Most executives spend 70–80% of their energy on coordination, sending updates, and reactive administration. When that drops, even by 20–30%, something profound happens: You think more. You frame better questions. You kill weak ideas earlier. You see patterns before others do. Your creative-to-administration ratio shifts. In practice, I've seen leaders double their creative judgment work from 20% to 40% within weeks.

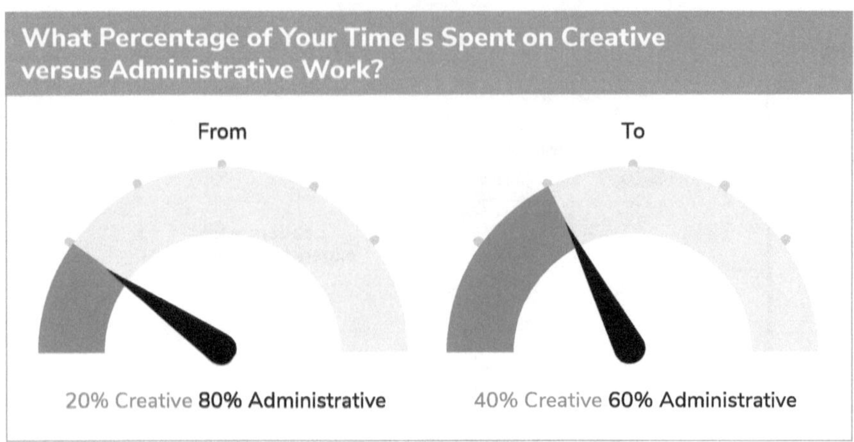

That shift alone transforms how leadership feels and how leaders show up. That's not just about wellbeing. That's about leverage.

AI-augmented leadership first delivers productivity. Then it accelerates performance. Finally, it enables presence, which sustains the leader, their teams, and the organization.

This Was Never About Tools

If there's one foundational principle to remember, it's this: **Do not start with tools.**

Start with who you are at your best, your strongest natural traits. Next, focus on the tasks where your judgment truly matters. Only then decide which tools align with your traits and tasks to best support you, and slowly build your AI stack.

Traits → Tasks → Tools

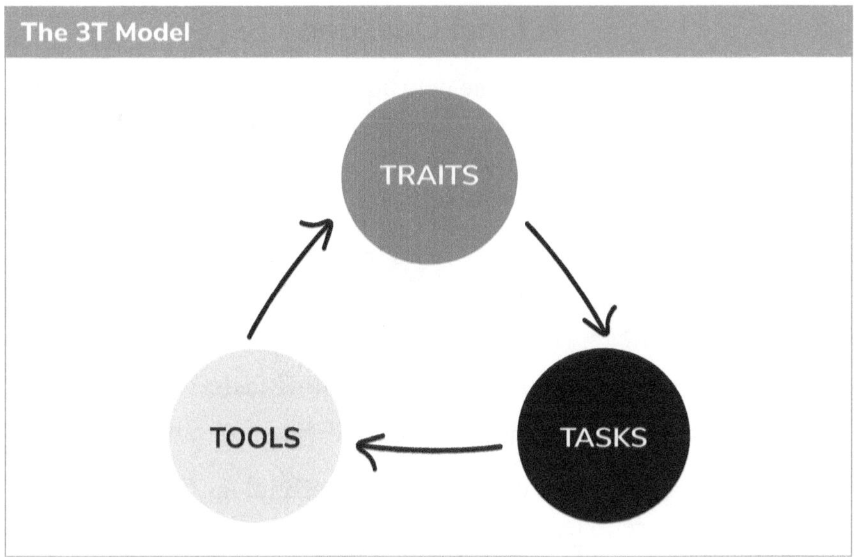

When leaders invert that order, they amplify noise. When they respect it, AI becomes a multiplier.

Your Legacy Will Be Defined by What You Unlearn

Here's the truth most executives don't hear often enough: Your legacy won't be defined by what you know. It will be defined by how willing you are to unlearn: to let go of practices that once made you successful but now limit you, to replace certainty with curiosity, to model learning instead of protecting identity.

Leaders who embrace AI as a genuine thinking partner—who integrate it into how they sense, think, decide, and act—will become exponentially more valuable over time. Those who don't won't just fall behind. They'll become irrelevant—not because they lack experience but because the world will keep moving, and they won't. When it comes to AI, there is no neutral position. Inaction is a decision.

A Final Question

The future will not reward those who adopt the most AI. It will reward leaders who build the fastest, clearest judgment systems, and stay unmistakably human while they do it.

Pause for a moment. Ask yourself:

- Where will I personally use AI to improve how I think?
- What routine work am I still protecting that no longer deserves my attention?
- What learning will I model so others move faster?
- What am I finally ready to unlearn—deliberately and visibly?

Artificial organizations don't start with technology. They start with leaders who choose to lead differently.

The systems that brought you here will not carry you forward. The age of intelligence waits for no one.

One question remains: **What kind of leader will you choose to be?**

ABOUT THE AUTHOR

Barry O'Reilly is an entrepreneur, executive advisor, and bestselling author who works with senior leaders to redesign how their organizations perform, make decisions, and innovate at scale.

He is the co-founder of Nobody Studios, a global Top 10 AI venture studio building and launching 100 companies in five years—applying venture-speed experimentation to de-risk new business creation before significant capital is deployed.

Barry is the author of *Lean Enterprise: How High Performance Organizations Innovate at Scale*—part of Eric Ries's Lean Series and recognized by *Harvard Business Review* as a must-read for CEOs—and *Unlearn: Let Go of Past Success to Achieve Extraordinary Results*, a repeatable system that enables leaders to surface legacy behaviors, replace outdated assumptions, and build the capabilities required to perform under uncertainty.

His work is grounded in enterprise transformation and venture-scale execution. He serves as faculty at Singularity University, contributes to *The Economist*, and advises boards and executive teams of global, high-growth and established organizations.

To learn more about Barry, visit barryoreilly.com.

To join the community and access best practices, templates, and additional tools, visit artificialorganizations.com.